Thomas Austin Dyson

Lives of some of the sons of St. Dominic

first series

Thomas Austin Dyson

Lives of some of the sons of St. Dominic
first series

ISBN/EAN: 9783741193149

Manufactured in Europe, USA, Canada, Australia, Japa

Cover: Foto ©Andreas Hilbeck / pixelio.de

Manufactured and distributed by brebook publishing software (www.brebook.com)

Thomas Austin Dyson

Lives of some of the sons of St. Dominic

LIVES

OF SOME OF THE

SONS OF ST. DOMINIC

FIRST SERIES.

BY

A FATHER OF THE SAME ORDER,

AUTHOR OF

THE LIFE OF ST. THOMAS AQUINAS.

NEW YORK:
D. & J SADLIER & COMPANY
31 BARCLAY STREET.
MONTREAL: 275 NOTRE DAME ST.
1883

APPROBATIONS.

Nos infrascripti Revisores Ord. Prad. pro scriptis excudendis fidem facimus quod perlectum opusculum cujus titulum, "Sons of Saint Dominic, First Series, by a Dominican Father" compilatum, typis mandari posse censemus. In quorum fidem his propria manu subscripsimus, Benetia, die 20 Decembris, 1882.

Fr. MANNES DOOGAN, O. P.
Fr. ANTONINUS ROONEY, O. P

Imprimatur,
    Fr. SADOC VILARRASA,
        Com. Gen. Calif. O. P.

After a careful examination of "The Lives of some of the Sons of Saint Dominic," published by Messrs. D. & J. Sadlier & Co., we approve of the same, and commend it to the Catholic public.

Very Rev. D. LILLY,
Provincial.

Imprimatur,
    ✠ JOHN CARDINAL MCCLOSKEY,
        Archbishop of New York.

July 25. 1883.

PREFACE.

THESE short Lives of some of the Saints of the Order of Saint Dominic are chiefly intended for Dominican Tertiaries. But it is thought that they will serve as beautiful examples of Christian virtues for those who are not in any way connected with the Order.

They are all compiled from authentic sources, mostly from the Bollandists. Some of them have already been printed in Catholic magazines and newspapers.

J. A. D.

INDEX.

	PAGE
BLESSED JORDAN OF SAXONY,	9
BLESSED ANTONY NEYROT,	71
BLESSED JAMES OF ULM,	87
BLESSED GILES OF SANTAREM,	113
BLESSED BERTRAND OF GARRIGUE	157
THE VENERABLE BARTHOLOMEW OF THE MARTYRS,	175
THE VENERABLE LEWIS OF GRANADA,	243

BLESSED JORDAN OF SAXONY.

SECOND MASTER-GENERAL OF THE ORDER OF FRIAR-PREACHERS.

CHAPTER I.

BLESSED JORDAN was born in the year 1190, in the little German town of Borrentrick, in the diocese of Paderborn. He was of the noble family of the Counts of Ebernstein.*

Nothing certain has come down to us about his early days, but, in the absence of anything to the contrary, we may suppose that he made his preparatory studies in his native country, most likely in the neighboring town of Paderborn, which had a flourishing school at that time. At any rate, we find him, when as yet quite

---

*Some authors say that he was born in Palestine while his parents were making a pilgrimage to the holy places, and that he was called Jordan, after the river in which our Lord was baptized. The name of Jordan, however, is probably derived from a German word, Gorden, to gird oneself with a belt.

young, at Paris, to complete his studies. It was usual at that time for a student who aspired to eminence, to study in that famous university, and among the students gathered there from all parts of Europe, those of Germany shone among the brightest. Jordan then, being of noble family, and having already shown signs of great talents, was sent by his parents to Paris. He advanced quickly, and in due time obtained the degree of Bachelor of Theology.

The life of a Parisian student was beset with many temptations; freed from the restraints of home, it was not to be wondered at if many wandered from the paths of virtue, and authors of the period describe in graphic terms the low state of morals among the students. But Jordan passed through this great trial unhurt. In the midst of the temptations to which he was necessarily exposed, and in spite of a natural tendency in his character to seek the love of all he met, so often a snare to the young, he lived a life of virginal purity.

He frequented the churches, and practiced the Christian virtues in great perfection, his charity to the poor being especially remarkable. Never did the indigent apply to him in vain, although, as he himself tells us, he was by no means rich. He made a holy resolution to give an alms every day to the first poor person he met, even though he were not asked. A very beautiful anecdote of his charity is told us. He always arose at midnight to assist at the Office of Matins in the cathedral of Notre Dame, but, as Gerard de Frachet, the author of the precious little book, "Vitæ Fratrum,"* tells us, on the night of a great feast he suddenly started out of sleep, thinking that the bell had already rung for the office, and that he was too late. In his haste he threw on a cloak, and fastening a girdle round his waist, set out for the cathedral. Whilst he

---

* Father Gerard de Frachet was born at Chaluz, near Limoges, and received the Dominican habit at Paris, November 11th, 1225. He was professed by Blessed Jordan on the feast of the Annunciation in the following year. He was successively Prior of Limoges (1233-1245), Marseilles, Provincial of Provence (1251-1258), Prior of Montpellier (1259-1266), and died at Limoges, October 4th, 1271.

He wrote the "Lives of the Brothers," by order of Blessed Humbert, Master-General of the Order, who in the General Chapter of Paris, 1256, ordered the Provincials of the various provinces to send him memoirs of all the Brothers and Fathers who had been remarkable for holiness of life, and gave the materials they collected to Father Gerard, then Provincial of Provence, for his book. He finished it in the year 1260. It has been printed twice—at Douay, in 1619, and at Valentia, in Spain, in 1657. A French translation also appeared in the "Annee Dominicaine" for 1874-1877. He also wrote a chronicle, from the beginning of the world until his own times, which, however, has not been published.

hurried along the deserted streets in the calm of the night, a solitary beggar asked his charity. Not having brought his purse with him, he took off his belt, which, according to the fashion of the times, was most likely ornamented with gold and precious stones, and gave it to the man. Coming to the cathedral he found he was too soon, and that the bell had not yet rung. He waited until the doors were opened, and, having entered, knelt in prayer before an image of our Blessed Lord crucified. When he had contemplated it some time, he saw that the belt, of which he had deprived himself for the love of God, was hung upon the crucifix, our Blessed Lord thus wishing to return it to him, and at the same time to show him how dear his charity had been to God.

CHAPTER II.

ST. DOMINIC being in Paris in the year 1219, Blessed Jordan became acquainted with him. We know not how their friendship began, but we know that these two beautiful souls understood and loved each other from the first, and, if we judge from the many marks of love in the writings of Blessed Jordan when speaking of St. Dominic, few could have loved him as he did, and have been so tenderly loved by St. Dominic. "I knew him familiarly," he says. He confessed to St. Dominic, and it was by his advice that he was ordained deacon.

But he did not make up his mind to enter the Dominican Order, until the preaching of Blessed Reginald of Orleans captivated his heart. This holy and celebrated religious, having consolidated the newly-founded convent of Bologna, was sent by St. Dominic to do the same work in the convent of St. Jacques at Paris. His success was almost miraculous; when he preached, the streets were deserted, and many of the students threw themselves into his arms, repented of their sins, and found a haven of rest in the white-robed ranks of Mary's Friars. Jordan tells us himself how he made up his mind to become a Dominican. "Blessed Reginald of happy memory," he says, "having come to Paris, and preaching there with great power, I was touched by grace, and made a vow within myself to enter his Order, for I thought I had found there a new road to salvation." And then he goes on to tell us how, in the fullness of his heart, he desired the same happiness for his friend, Henry of Cologne, one of the most endearing of the early sons of St. Dominic. They were familiarly united in the sweet bonds of holy christian love, lodged in the same house, and followed the same course of studies. When quite young, Henry had been nominated Canon of Utrecht, and had been brought up in the fear and love of God by one of the Canons of that cathedral, a man of great piety and prudence, who, by example as well as by precept, had taught him to overcome the world by crucifying his flesh, and by the practice of good works. He caused him frequently to wash the feet of the poor, to attend the beautiful services of the church, to flee all evil as he would a pest, to scorn luxury, and, above all, to love the angelic virtue of chastity, so that this youth, being of good natural qualities, became very docile under the yoke of virtue. He is described by the early historians of the Order as an angelic youth, gracious in all things. Blessed Jordan thus paints him in vivid colors: "He was prompt in obedience, firm in patience, calm in gentleness, pleasing in cheerfulness, abundant in charity; nor were nobility of manners, sincerity of heart and virginal integrity in the flesh wanting to him." "There was in him," he says, "modesty in his words, acuteness of wit, beauty of face, comeliness of person, ease in writing, skill in dictating, and a voice of angelic sweetness. No one ever saw him sad or in a hurry, he was always even in spirit, always cheerful." What could be added to this charming sketch of Henry of Cologne, whom every one loved, but none so much as Jordan. "A man," he says in another place, "whom I loved in Christ, with an affection I never gave to any other."

Blessed Henry having come to Paris, made the acquaintance of Jordan, and these two chosen souls became fast friends. "I began," Jordan continues, "to desire to bind by the same vow (to enter the Order) the companion and love of my soul, in whom I saw all the qualifications of nature and grace required for a preacher. He refused me, but I ceased not to press him. I so brought it about that he should confess to Blessed Reginald, and receive godly exhortations from him. On his return from Blessed Reginald to me, opening the Prophet Isaias, he lit upon the following words: 'The Lord hath given me a learned tongue, that I should know how to uphold by word him that is weary.' (Isa., chap. 50, v. 4.) I interpreted these words as a voice from heaven to enter religion; we saw some lines lower down—'Let us stand together.' (Isa., chap. 50, v. 8.) They seemed to say to us that we should not be separated." The same night Jordan went to Matins in the church of Our Blessed Lady, and stayed after the Office until dawn, praying to the Mother of God to change the heart of his friend, and to give him an ardent desire for a life of voluntary poverty, obedience and chastity.

The answer to his prayers was a terrible vision, which Blessed Henry saw in his sleep. He dreamed that he saw our Blessed Lord seated on His throne judging all men. One of the crowd, turning his face full upon Henry, said to him, "And thou who standest there, what hast thou abandoned for God's sake?" A short but agonizing struggle took place in his heart after he awoke. He could resist no longer, and, seeking Blessed Reginald, he made a vow in his hands to enter the Order.

"He came to find me," continues Jordan's narrative, "and while I looked at the traces of tears upon his angelic face, I asked him where he had been. He answered: 'I have made a vow to the Lord and will keep it.' Nevertheless, we put off taking the habit until Lent, and, in the meanwhile, gained one of our companions, Brother Leo," who afterwards succeeded Blessed Henry as Prior of Cologne.

Blessed Reginald died before they entered the Order; but the day having come, when our holy Mother the Church reminds all men of their lowly origin by sprinkling ashes upon their heads; these three fervent disciples of Christ went to the Dominican church of St. Jacques, and entered just at the moment when the Friars sang the antiphon "*Immutemur habitu.*" Their arrival was unexpected, yet welcome, and Jordan and his two companions casting off their secular dress were clothed in the beautiful white habit of St. Dominic. This was in the year 1220, when Jordan was thirty years of age. His entrance into the ranks of the Friar Preachers drew many other students of note, among whom was Everard, Archdeacon of Lausanne, who a short time before had refused the Bishopric of that town; and his example, in its turn, drew many others.

At the death of Blessed Reginald, Jordan had a marvellous vision. He saw a limpid stream flow from its source, which, after a time, disappeared, and in its place sprang forth from the earth two other streams, which spread themselves into all parts of the earth, ever and ever increasing, until they threw themselves into the sea. The first stream which sank into the bowels of the earth was interpreted by Jordan to mean Blessed Reginald, who had just then died; one of the other streams he applied to Blessed Henry, and we, in our turn, knowing his subsequent life, interpret the third one to mean Jordan himself, for, like a mighty river, his apostolic voice penetrated for seventeen years into all parts of Europe, drawing above one thousand novices into the Order, until having finished his earthly course, he threw himself into the unfathomable sea of that blessed eternity —the bosom of God.

CHAPTER III.

JORDAN had been a novice only about three months when he was called to the first General Chapter of the Dominican Order, held at Bologna, at Pentecost of the year 1220. On his return from Paris, he was charged by his superiors to teach Holy Scripture to the novices, and it is probable that the commentary on the gospel of St. Luke, which he published, was the first of his labors at that time. He was also employed in preaching, and soon became popular. He was so persuasive that no one could resist him; in fact, this gift of persuasion was his peculiar characteristic. Not only in his sermons, but also in private conversation, he spoke so eloquently, and explained and enforced his ideas by so appropriate examples, and suited himself so perfectly to the wants of his hearers, that he invariably produced conviction in their minds and moved their hearts. But it was upon students and young men that his sermons had most effect. There were about thirty or forty thousand students in Paris at that time. They were distinguished by birth and rank, some rich in fiefs, others in ecclesiastical benefices, learned in all branches of knowledge. Many of these, vanquished by the irrepressible sweetness of Jordan, renounced all for Jesus, and were clothed in the habit of the Friar Preachers.

The Dominican Order held its second General Chapter at Bologna, in the following year, 1221. It was the last at which St. Dominic presided. Blessed Jordan was not present, but was appointed Provincial of Lombardy by the Fathers who had met together. "In 1221," he says, "in the Chapter of Bologna, they thought fit to impose upon me the office of Provincial of the Province of Lombardy. I had only passed a year in the Order. Before I had time to take root, as was necessary for me, they put me at the head of others, *I* who had not yet learned how to guide myself in the work of my own salvation." The Fathers of the Chapter sent word to him to set out at once to take his new office, and at the same time ordered his dear friend Henry to set out to become Prior of Cologne, and thus, after one short year of brotherhood in the Order, these two friends were separated, although they had hoped to have passed their whole lives together.

Jordan set out immediately for his province. He was accompanied by a religious whom he loved much. This was Brother Everard, of whom we have already spoken, who undertook this journey from a double motive: "moved by the desire," says Blessed Humbert de Romanis, the fifth General of the Order, "to see the Blessed Father Dominic, and also by his love for Master Jordan." His wish to see St. Dominic was not realized upon this earth, for the holy Patriarch died August 5th, at Bologna, while Brother Everard lay upon his death-bed at Lausanne, where he had been chosen Bishop but a short time before.

Leaving the death-bed of this, his dear friend and disciple, Jordan continued his journey, and arrived at Bologna, only to find that St. Dominic had died some days before.

From a deed executed by Blessed Jordan, we

know that he was in that city on the eighteenth of August of that year. All the Friars were in great fear; they dreaded, having lost their Father and founder, and having no longer a common head, being forced to disperse. And at the same time they were subjected to severe trials from the old enemy of souls, who, gaining courage after the death of St. Dominic, now began to revenge himself upon his children by possessing their bodies and disturbing their peace of mind, chiefly by horrible visions in the night. Blessed Jordan consoled them, and after having, to some extent, restored calm, proceeded on his way to Lombardy.

He only remained Provincial of that province long enough to show what eminent powers of government he possessed; for in the third General Chapter, held May 22, 1222, at Paris, he was chosen by the voice of the whole Order, to be the successor of St. Dominic. And thus, after little more than two years in the ranks of the Friars of Mary, as the Friar Preachers were commonly called, he was chosen for their head.

No more striking proof of the high estimation in which he was held could have been paid him.

In his new sphere of labor as Master-General, "his chief care," says Blessed Humbert, "was to increase the Order, with a view to the salvation of souls; for this end he set himself to attract the learned, fixing his abode, from choice, in the cities where there were scholars." It was also to this end that he obtained for his Order two public chairs of Theology in the University of Paris. "In those days." continues Blessed Humbert, "the Order gradually increased in provinces, convents and religious." From contemplation flowed the apostolate, the natural consequence of fervor of soul and solid doctrine. "God," says Father Gerard de Frachet, "shed an admirable fervor upon the teaching of the Friars," and this fervor drew numbers of souls into their ranks. Blessed Jordan alone is said to have clothed more than a thousand novices with his own hands. In 1226 he writes from Paris: "I have received twenty-one novices in the space of four months." During the Lent of 1227 he clothed thirty at Bologna, and his letters, some of which have been handed down to our own days, are full of such like experiences. He was so certain of attracting students into the Order, that on arriving at any convent he caused a number of habits to be made ready, and very often his success so exceeded his hopes, that the poor procurators of the convent were at their wits end to find clothes for all who came. Once on the Feast of Pentecost he clothed twenty-one young men in the Dominican habit, "when," says the old writer, "there were many tears that day, for on one side the Friars wept for joy, and on the other the seculars from grief to see the flower of their families thus snatched from the world." One of them, a German, on account of his youth, had often been refused by Blessed Jordan. But he stole in among the others who were to be clothed. Jordan saw his plot at once, but thought it hard to turn him away in the presence of about a thousand students who had come to see the ceremony, so he said in a low voice: "One of you steals the Order from us." Now, the vestiarian had only brought twenty-one habits, and not being able to go to seek for another, on account of the crowd, this young man received a tunic from one, a scapular from another, and so obtained the whole habit from the charity of those present. He afterwards became a Lector of Theology, and a famous preacher. Upon another occasion several students had gone to be witnesses of the reception of one of their number. Jordan thus spoke to them: "If one of you were to go to a great feast, would the others be so careless as not to wish to go with him? Well, my friends, this youth is bidden to a great feast by the authority of God, will you let him enter alone?" And his words had no sooner fallen from his lips, than a student, who, up till that moment had no thought of becoming a religious, came forward and said: "Master, I come at your voice to join myself to this youth, in the name of Jesus Christ," and both of them received the habit at the same time.

Yet another example of these beautiful vocations, for the old chronicles of the Order are full of them. One of his most precious conquests was a young German, as remarkable for his innocence of heart, as for his high rank. His tutor and friends, seeing him ready to quit the pleasures of this world, at the voice of Jordan, engaged the ministers of Satan to hinder him, and introduced a very beautiful courtesan into his room, who they hoped would turn him from his pious intention. But by the grace of God he conquered, and his tutor was so much struck by his fortitude, that he afterwards followed his example and became a Dominican. But his rich and powerful father, when he learnt that his only son had become a poor Friar, went with a numerous retinue from Germany to Padua, with the firm intention of dragging his son back with him, or, if he failed in that, at least to put an end to Master Jordan. Arriving in the town, he met the saint by accident, and in an imperious voice asked him where he could find Master Jordan. Remembering how our Blessed Lord had answered the Jews who wished to kill him—"It is I," Jordan said with a joyful voice, and with a heart full of humility, "I am Master Jordan." This calm and frankness, and the grace of God knocking at his heart, conquered the German lord. He alighted from his horse, and in the face of all his followers, who well knew his previous intention, threw himself at the feet of Jordan, and confessed, with tears in his eyes, the evil design he had nourished in his heart.

CHAPTER IV.

JORDAN showed in a very striking manner that he had all the qualifications necessary for governing the Order. The old lives are full of praises of the way in which he carried out his duties as Father General. But, above all, he succeeded in gaining the love of those whom God had placed under his care. "The sweet Father Jordan" is the usual term applied to him by his biographers. *Dulcis Pater Jordanus*, and they always class him with St. Dominic as the co-founder of the Dominican Order; for, in truth, Jordan built up what Dominic had begun. Thus one writer, when speaking of the first days of the Order, says: "In the times of our holy Father St. Dominic and Master Jordan, the fervor of the Brothers was such that it was impossible to describe it." His gentleness and care for the Brothers were very great; he not only showed compassion for their infirmities—and who is not weak?—but also was very prudent and merciful in pardoning the faults of human frailty. This he did not so much by severity, although none knew better than he how to be unflinching in due time and place, as by persuasion and sweetness. But his tenderness and compassion were principally for those Brothers who were tempted; he consoled those by his presence, animated them to resist temptation by his words, and to persevere in the vocation the good God had given them.

When he arrived at any convent it was his custom to call for the novices to speak to them about the state of their souls. Thus arriving one day at Paris, he found that one of the novices was tempted to leave the Order, "and the sweet Father Jordan," as the old chronicle has it, set himself to examine him, and to help him to overcome the temptation. But all his words and efforts having been in vain, the youth still wishing to return into the world, and demanding his secular clothes and all he had brought with him, the Master told him he should, without fail, leave on the morrow. The next day being Pentecost, all the community having made the usual procession, entered the Chapter room, and the Master called the novice before him. He warned him gently of the fatal consequences of throwing away his vocation, and earnestly entreated him not to listen to the voice of the evil one, who thus trusted to gain possession of his soul. But seeing all he could say made no impression upon his heart, he sent him at last to the Vestiary to ask for his worldly dress. Then, when he had gone, he turned to the Fathers and Brothers and said to them: "Let us kneel and say the '*Veni Creator Spiritus.*'" They had not ended the hymn when the door of the Chapter room opened, and the novice entered, threw himself on his knees, and asked pardon for his fault, promising with tears of repentance in his eyes to persevere for the future. The Fathers, filled with joy, not unmixed with holy fear, thanked God for this soul thus snatched from such danger, and readily granted him pardon; and we read that he, who had so nearly given way in the hour of trial, made swift progress in knowledge and virtue, so that in time he became a Lector of Theology, and a preacher whose words led many to God.

Arriving once at Bologna, the Fathers spoke to him of another novice tempted in the same way. He had led a very delicate life in regard to his food and amusements, and in short he had never known pain or affliction, with the sole exception of the labor necessary for his studies, in which he shone brightly. He had never been ill, and knew not what sorrow was. He had fasted but once a year on Good Friday, and rarely abstained from meat. He had never confessed, and was so ignorant of prayer that the "Our Father" was the only one he knew Having gone to the Dominican Convent, from curiosity to see what the life of the Brothers of the new Order was like, he was so pleased with what he saw, that he asked to be admitted as a novice. The Fathers accepted him, and, on account of the natural openness of his character, loved him much.

However, he soon grew weary of a life of penance and prayer, and began to yearn for the pleasures of the world which he had so lately given up for the love of God. Everything in the daily routine of the convent was displeasing to him; he could neither eat nor sleep, and it seemed to him as if he had condemned himself to a life of death, while yet living in this world. His temper soured, and although he had never been angry before his entrance into religion, temptation had made him so touchy that he even threatened to strike the sub-Prior.

The poor Fathers spoke to Blessed Jordan about him. Our saint sent for and consoled him, then led him to the altar of St. Nicholas, and bade him kneel and say the Lord's Prayer. Then placing his hands upon his head, he prayed to God, with all the fervor of his soul, to take away this temptation from him. While he prayed thus, the novice felt an inexpressible sweetness enter his soul, it seemed to him, as he afterwards told two of the Fathers, as if a great pressure was removed from his heart, and he fell into a great calm and peace of soul. He afterwards became remarkable for his fervor and love of God, and labored long and fruitfully in the vineyard of the Lord.

All troubled and afflicted souls obtained consolation from Master Jordan. A certain Brother was much tempted to desolation of spirit. One day Jordan found him saying the Office of the Dead, and seated himself silently beside him; then he bagan to say the Office with him, verse by verse. When the poor Brother said that verse of the psalm, "I believe to see the good things of the Lord in the land of the living," (Psalm 26, v. 13), Jordan devoutly answered in his turn, emphasizing each word, "Expect the Lord, do manfully and let thy heart take courage, and wait then for the Lord;" and at this application of the words of the psalm to the hidden state of his soul, the Brother felt himself refreshed, and at once the temptation left him, never to return.

He was also very merciful to those who had been so unhappy as to fall into sin, and labored with his whole soul to restore them to the grace of God. One of the Friars had left the Order, forgetting his vow of obedience. Jordan wished him to return, and ably pleaded for him before several of the Fathers met together to consider the case. With one sole exception, they came round to his side, but this Father obstinately refused his consent. "He is, without doubt, guilty of grave sin," remonstrated Father Jordan, "but what will become of him if we abandon him?" The Father answered that it was no affair of his. Then the sweet Father Jordan, whom the hardness of this answer touched to the quick, cried out: "If you, my dear Brother, had shed but one drop of your blood for this poor man, as Jesus Christ has shed all of his, for us, you would never speak thus." The Father covered with shame, seeing his fault, threw himself upon the ground, begged pardon for the scandal he had caused, and gave his consent.

CHAPTER V.

FEW men of that time traveled more than Jordan. The General Chapters of the Order were held every year in Bologna and Paris, in turn; and his life, after his election as Master-General, passed almost entirely in journeying to and fro between these two cities, varied occasionally by journeys into Germany. Some of his letters have been handed down to us, and from these we can gather an idea of his apostolic wanderings. Thus in the year 1223, he left Bologna and commenced a journey which would bring him, in the end, to Paris, for the General Chapter was to be held in that city on the seventh of July of the year following. From his letters we find that he first went to Venice with his two companions, Fathers John and Archangel. Then we find him in the university town of Padua, where he preached; at first he drew but one scholar into the Order, but after a little while they came more abundantly, attracted by the beauty of his character, and the charm of his words, so that he was able to write to his spiritual daughter, Blessed Diana, that he had clothed ten, and before he left he had given the habit to thirty-three, among whom was the famous Albert the Great. We next hear of him at Brescia, in the month of August, where he was laid up some time with the fever; then at Milan, Besancon, and towards All Saints Day in Paris. He stayed in Paris until after the Chapter, and then left to return to Bologna, where he preached the Lent, 1225.

After the Chapter of Bologna, in the same year, 1225, he started for Germany, accompanied on the first part of the way by the German Dominicans who had taken part in the Chapter, among whom was his dear friend, Henry of Cologne. Their intention was to enter Germany by the Tyrolese Alps. Verona and Trent were on their way. In the first of these towns he was again attacked by the fever. After his recovery he went on to Trent, from whence he writes to Blessed Diana, who had heard of his illness, to remove her fears. He says in this letter that he left Verona on St. Laurence's Day, August 10th, and that he preached at Trent on the Feast of the Assumption, August 15th, to the people, and to the clergy of the town on the following day. From Trent he proceeded to Magdeburg, where he arrived on the 24th of September, then to Treves and Cologne, being just in time to assist at the death-bed of Blessed Henry, who had left him at Magdeburg, in order to reach his convent by a shorter route.

He thus describes this sad event in another letter to Blessed Diana: "I wept," he says, "and do yet weep for my sweet friend, and I mourn for my most amiable Brother. I weep for a well-beloved son, Brother Henry, Prior of Cologne. He passed happily to his fatherland, and has left me in the midst of this perverse world. But I have not been the only one to weep. What shall I say of the tears shed by all the citizens of Cologne? What of the lamentations, and, above all, by the Brothers, holy virgins and widows?" Farther on he says: "We have not lost him, but he has gone before to heaven.

Oh, let us follow him, let us haste, in our turn, to enter into unending rest."

"The feast of St. Severin (October 23d), was the day of his heavenly birth," he thus continues, "and he, leaving this life, died to the world, but was born to God. The night of October 23d, as soon as the bell had rung for Matins, I went to see him before going to choir Having found him gasping for breath, and already in his last agony, I asked him if he wished to receive Extreme Unction, he answered that he earnestly desired it. We wished to carry out his desires before saying Matins. He seemed rather to give himself the Sacrament than to receive it from others, for he said the prayers most devoutly. After the Unction we went down to the choir, and said the Office of nine lessons in honor of St. Severin, patron of Cologne. I was struck with their meaning, and inwardly applied them to our Henry, who was on the point of entering into Heaven. Immediately my eyes were filled with tears; they fell in torrents, and I experienced an inexpressible calm. Having returned I found him speaking of God, and to God, in transports of joy, singing, inciting himself and the others to the desire of the heavenly land, full of distaste of this sad place of exile, consoling the Fathers who stood around, and saying to them: 'O my Fathers, my soul is dilated upon you.' At these words his soul started up, he began to sing, and to repeat often and tenderly this invocation: 'Holy Virgin, make us worthy of this heavenly bread.'

"He then said to those, who already shone like stars in the sky and like torches in the world: 'The Lord has chosen you for his inheritance.' It was with such and other like words, by desire of death and by exhortations to live holily, that this blessed soul prepared to depart. At the moment when the Lord called him, and when were already begun the attacks of the enemy who tries to bruise our heel, he repeated these words of Jacob: 'God shall be with me, and shall keep me in the way by which I walk, and shall give me bread to eat, and raiment to put on. And I shall return prosperously to my Father's house, and the Lord shall be my God,' (Genesis, chap. 28, v. 20–21) 'and the Cross of Christ my standard.'

"He continued some time thus, and added: 'The prince of this world draws near, but he will be powerless against me.' After saying these and other words no less remarkable, he entered into his agony, and we began to make the recommendation of his soul, to moan and weep. Our prayers were broken by sobs, and sometimes interrupted by a mournful silence."

After the death of this, his dearest friend on earth, Jordan continued his journey to Paris, and presided at the General Chapter held in that city, June 7, 1226.

These journeys give us some idea of how his life was spent. But his wanderings were not confined to journeys to and fro between Paris and Bologna; he went as far as England. In the year 1230, a quarrel having arisen between the townsmen and the students of Paris, the course of studies was stopped, and many thousands of students crossed the channel to study at Oxford. Jordan went also, and while there received many learned Englishmen into the Order, among whom was Robert Bacon, then an old man full of knowledge and holiness, and

Richard Fishacre, who was so dear to Bacon that he could not part from him. He was the first English Dominican who commentated on the Book of Sentences of Peter Lombard.

Many beautiful anecdotes are told of these journeys. Thus we read that when traveling he was accustomed to spend the whole of his time in prayer, at least when not speaking to the Brothers who accompanied him. Sometimes, as he walked along the road, he sang the hymn "*Jesu Nostra Redemptio*," or the "*Salve Regina;*" sometimes, all absorbed in devotion and inward joy, he strayed from the road and lost his way, but no one ever saw him troubled about it; on the contrary, he consoled his companions. "Be calm," he would say, "there is but one road about which we should be anxious—the road to heaven."

Passing once from Lombardy into Germany, he came to a village among the mountains called Ursatia. He had with him two Friars and a secular clerk, who, later on, joined the Order. Overcome with fatigue, and famishing for food, they went into an inn, kept by a man called Untha, and asked him to prepare them something to eat. He answered that he could not, for several travelers had passed that way already and had eaten all he had, except two loaves, which he had laid aside for himself and his family. The Father answered: "Serve us what you have because we are in urgent need of food." Then the host brought the two loaves, which, in truth, were of the smallest, and Blessed Jordan having blessed them, began to give them away in pieces to the poor, who, hearing of the arrival of strangers had come together in the hope of getting an alms. This appeared very singular conduct to the inn-keeper, who cried out in haste: "What are you doing? Have you forgotten that no more bread can be had here, and that the doors have been purposely shut to hinder the poor from coming in?" But for his whole answer Jordan ordered the doors to be opened still wider, and calmly continued his alms. Now, the number of the poor was about thirty, and to each of them he gave so large a piece, that what one received would have been sufficient for all, yet he and his companions satisfied their hunger, and there remained a goodly quantity for the host and his family. Untha seeing this miracle, said: "Truly this man is a saint of God," and he refused to take any payment, but gave a flask of wine to the secular clerk to help them on their way.

Traveling in France he was one day received by a pious lady, whose husband, however, was not at all inclined to hospitality, especially towards Religious. Blessed Jordan and his companions were seated at table with the lady, when her husband came in. He took his place with a bad grace, not being pleased to find them there, and kept a dogged silence, thus wishing to show them that they were his guests by no will of his. After a while the servants brought a very choice wine, and enraged by this mark of attention to men he disliked, he said to the servants: "Go quickly and get some better wine than this; bring that which is in such a place in the cellar," indicating a particular barrel which he knew was so sour that it was no longer good enough to drink, and this he did on purpose to annoy his wife, and to vent his spleen on the Friars.

The servants did as they were bid, and brought the wine; but, contrary to his wishes, it was excellent. The master of the house, beside himself with rage, said: "Why have you not drawn from the barrel I told you of?" The servant answered that he had done so, and went again, but with the same result. Then the man, whose passion was now ungovernable, went down himself into the cellar, tasted the wine from the barrel, and found it excellent. Then, seeing the miracle which God had worked to show the sanctity of his guest, he completely changed, and he who, up till then, had chid his wife for her hospitality to the Friars, now went beyond her in his love for them, and even urged her on to give them alms.

The following beautiful incident shows us that even the mute beasts obeyed the voice of Jordan. "One day," says Father Gerard de Frachet, "the Master left Lausanne to pay a visit to the bishop of that town, who lived in the neighborhood. These two souls for a long time had cherished for each other a very holy affection. Several Friars led the way, and the Blessed followed in company with the sacristan of Lausanne, talking of Jesus. But a weasel having run across the road in front of the Brothers, who were a little in advance, they stopped and stood round the hole in which it had hid itself.

"The Master coming up, said: 'Why do you stop here?' 'Because,' they said, 'a very beautiful little animal has run into this hole.' Then the Master, bending towards the ground, said: 'Come out, pretty little beast, that we may look at you,' and immediately the weasel showed itself at the mouth of its hole, and fixed its eyes intently upon the Master, who took it into his hands and gently stroked it upon the back. Then he let it go with these words: 'Return now into your tiny house, and may God, your Maker, be blessed forever.' It obeyed and instantly disappeared."

CHAPTER VI.

THIS great servant of God practiced the Christian virtues in great perfection. We will try to give some account of them, although we know well that words fall far short of the truth when speaking of the saints of God, and of the marvels He works in their souls. The charity and compassion towards the poor, of which he had given so many striking proofs when as yet a secular living in the world, were not lessened after his entrance into religion. He often gave his tunic from his back to clothe one of the needy ones of Christ. The Fathers reproved him for this in a General Chapter, but history is silent as to the effect. One day, deceived by a beggar, who pretended to be very poor, he gave him his tunic. The man immediately took it to a tavern to receive its value in drink. A Friar seeing this, said: "Master, see to what use he puts your alms." To whom Jordan answered: "If I have thus acted, it was because the miserable appearance of this man betokened a state of great poverty. To help him seemed to be an act of charity, and, indeed, I think it is better to lose a tunic than to lose charity."

He inherited the most beautiful trait in the character of our holy Father St. Dominic—that of holy joy. As he was once traveling with a number of Friars to Paris for the next General Chapter, he arrived at a little village about dinner time. He sent some of the Friars to seek some bread, telling them he would await their return beside a fountain on the road side. The Brothers came back with only one loaf, sufficient, perhaps, for four. Then the saint was in great joy. But a woman passing by was scandalized, seeing him and his companions so joyful. "Is it well," she said, "to be so mirthful thus early in the morning?" But when she learnt that the cause of their glee was the want of necessary things, and the exercise of holy poverty, she was much edified, and running quickly to her house brought them bread and cheese in abundance, begging their prayers.

He was so humble that he fled all the honors the world offered him. One day when he came near Bologna, learning that many of the citizens were coming out in procession to meet him, he contrived to make a tour of the town by little-known paths, and reached the Dominican Convent unseen. But it was above all in the General Chapters of the Order that his humility showed itself the most. Although he was the head and superior of all present, he submitted to, and even invited the reproofs of the Fathers. He was taken to task for something he had done, which had not pleased, and asked to excuse or explain his reasons for thus acting. "No," he said, "should one hear the excuses of a Brigand?" and all were much edified by his answer.

He wept so much for his sins, although his life was so pure and holy, blameless in all things, that he lost the sight of one eye, and in one of these Chapters he said: "My Fathers, thank God who has delivered me from an enemy, but ask Him, if it please Him, and is for my good, to preserve me the use of the other."

He practiced holy poverty strictly, and rejoiced in the hardships it imposed on him. He was held in the highest estimation by all, but especially by Pope Gregory IX., formerly Cardinal Ugolino, ever the warm friend of the Dominican Order. He once forced him to submit to the very rare honor of dining at the same table with himself. The same day Jordan left Rome for a visitation, and the night coming on, he was obliged to find some place of rest. He went to the house of the parish priest of a little village, who, taking him for an ordinary religious, would not receive him. A poor man at last took him in, but he was so needy that he could not give him any supper. This delighted Father Jordan, and he said to his companion: "Blessed be the priest, for by his rebuff he has made me expiate the honor of having been seated this day at table with the Supreme Pontiff."

He once received hospitality among the Cistercian monks. Standing around him, one of them said: "Master, how can your Order exist, being founded upon alms only? You know well, that although men appear to be pious and

Blessed Jordan of Saxony. 51

favorable to you now, yet that it is written in the holy gospels that the charity of many will become cold, and then you will no longer have any alms, and your Order will cease."

With all gentleness the Master answered him thus: "I will convince you, by your own words, that the Cistercian Order, in such a case, would be destroyed before ours. Read the passage of the gospels which you quote, and you will see that the charity of many will grow cold where iniquity abounds, and that intolerable persecutions will arise; these persecutors, tyrants, and all the evil-minded, will rob you of your temporal goods, and you who are not accustomed to go from one place to another to ask alms, will necessarily succumb. But our Brothers, although they will be dispersed, will produce greater fruit, like the Apostles, who were scattered abroad in times of persecution. Nor will our Brothers let themselves be frightened, but going two and two from town to town, according to their usual custom, will seek their bread. But I say more than this; that those who will despoil you, will voluntarily give to us, if **we** will receive from them, for it is a fact, of which we have daily experience, that spoliators and pillagers wish to give us, with joy, that which they have taken from others, if we would receive at their hands."

Blessed Jordan was gifted with a very rare spirit of retirement and recollection. The life of the soul alone occupied his thoughts, and all outward things were for him as if they were not, so much so, that his clothes were sometimes changed without his knowing it, as it happened one day when a pious man wishing to obtain something which the saint had worn, took his shoes, and put his own, which were highly ornamented, in their place. The Blessed did not notice any difference when he put them on, and, to the astonishment of all, appeared among the Friars with costly shoes on his feet.

God had also given him a special gift of prayer, so that no duty whatever could make him neglect it. His habitual manner was to pray kneeling, with joined hands and upright body; but sometimes he prayed seated.

But how can we describe his devotion to Mary

the Mother of God, for whom even careless Catholics have a constant love. He could not have been a worthy child of St. Dominic if he had not loved her with a love all special. Mary also loved him, and continued to favor the Dominican Order with the same special protection which she had shown it in the times of St. Dominic. We can never forget how she had taken the newly-founded band of fervent souls that holy saint had gathered together under her care, and we know that it is to Mary that the Friar preachers must look amid the trials of this world. Blessed Jordan knew this well, and, in truth, Mary did not let him forget it. Many times she showed herself visibly in the Dominican monasteries, as she had done in the days of St. Dominic.

Blessed Jordan once told the Fathers that a certain Friar, and no one doubted that he spoke of himself, on the feast of the Purification, when the Fathers sang the antiphon "*Ecce Venit,*" saw a beautiful lady leading her infant son by the hand, advance towards the altar, and take her place upon a throne prepared for her, from whence she looked upon the Brothers with mild and loving eyes, and when the long lines of Friars bent low at "*Gloria Patri,*" this beautiful Queen, for it was Mary, Queen of Angels and of men, took the little hand of her Divine Son, and with it made the sign of the Cross over them, after which the consoling vision faded away.

How beautiful is also the following incident: One night as Master Jordan was praying, according to his wont, before the altar of Mary, a Brother set himself to watch him. As the saint prayed he heard him say, from time to time, the first words of the "*Ave Maria.*" After a while Jordan found the Brother in darkness, and said to him: "Who are you?" "I am your son, Berthold," the novice answered. Then the Blessed Father said: "Go and rest yourself, my child." "No, Father," persisted the novice, "for I wish you now to explain to me how you pray." "The most sweet Father," as he is called, condescending to the desires of the young religious, then told him the way in which he prayed. It was a series of certain psalms and antiphons which begin with the letters of the name of

Mary, and which have come down to us under the name of the "Salutation of Blessed Jordan to the Most Holy Virgin," although he did not originate it, it having existed before his time. Having thus satisfied the pious desires of Brother Berthold, Jordan continued: "I wish to show you, by an example, how sweet and salutary it is to praise our Blessed Lady." And then he told him, without saying that it happened to himself, how our Lady, in a vision, said to a certain Brother Preacher: "I love this Order with a special love. Among other things it is most pleasing to me that you begin and end all your actions and sermons with my name. This is the reason why I have obtained a promise from my Son that no one shall ever remain in the Order in a state of mortal sin, for either his sin will be found out, or he will immediately repent, or he will be expelled, so that my Order may not be defiled."

But the most beautiful vestige of his love for Mary is the "*Salve Regina*," which the Dominican Fathers sing every evening after Complin. We have already alluded to the possession of the Brothers by evil spirits at Bologna, after the death of St. Dominic. Many other convents were also troubled in the same way. Ridiculous phantoms, unclean appearances in the night, and terrifying visions harassed and plagued the poor Friars, so that they were obliged to take in turn the duty of watching through the night to guard the convents from harm.

Jordan seeing that if these terrible temptations continued, many would be overcome and his Order be depopulated, ordered that after Mâtins the Brothers should sing the antiphon "*Te Sanctum,*" to invoke the help of the holy angels. But this not proving successful, he ordained that the "*Salve Regina*" should be sung every night in solemn procession after Complin, to implore the aid Mary never denies to those who pray to her. Then the temptations ceased. This custom was soon afterwards introduced into the whole Dominican Order, by the General Chapter of Paris, 1224, and continues to this day. Such was the origin of this touching ceremony, which all those who have seen it remember well, so simple, yet so beautiful, in the midst of this unlovely age, a link with the faith of our Catholic forefathers, and now, as ever, the buckler and sure defence of the Friar Preachers against the attacks of the enemy.

Blessed Jordan, although he was very gentle and much beloved by his sons in the Order, on account of his pity and tenderness for their shortcomings, yet could be bold, even in the face of the mighty ones of this earth, as the following anecdote shows us: He was once admitted to an audience with the Emperor Frederick II., who received him very graciously. They both sat, and for a long time were silent, the Emperor awed, perhaps, by the holiness of Jordan, and the holy religious pondering in his mind how he could best say what he knew was his duty to tell the Emperor, without offending him, and perhaps doing more harm than good. At last he said: "My Lord, the office I hold leads me into many provinces. I wonder, therefore, you do not ask me for some news." To whom the Emperor answered: "I have my agents in all my lands, and know well what is done in the world." "Yea, my Lord," persisted

Jordan, "but the Lord Jesus Christ, being God, knew all things, and yet asked his disciples: 'Whom do men say I am?' You are a man and ignorant of many things which are said of you, which, nevertheless, it behooves you to know. It is said of you that you burden churches, that you despise judgments, and that you pay attention to soothsayers, that you favor Jews and Saracens, that you do not honor the Vicar of Christ, the successor of St. Peter, who is the Father of all Christians and our spiritual Lord, and, in truth, all these things do not become you;" and in this way, and with many other such like words, he reproved him without offending him in the least.

CHAPTER VII.

IT was no wonder that the devil, seeing the holiness of this great servant of God, and the good he was working among the souls of men, tried to entrap him by subtle temptations. Once when he was at Paris, sick of the fever to which he was subject all his life, the malicious spirit, having taken the form of a respectable person, knocked at the gate of the convent, and asked to see Father Jordan. Admitted into his presence, he made a few commonplace remarks, after which, putting on a confidential air, he asked that the Brother who was present might retire, as he had some special business to transact with him. Then he said: "Master, you are at the head of a very holy order, and the eyes of all your Friars are turned towards you. All your acts, whether little or great, have an immense influence upon their fervor. Every irregularity therefore on your part will have its effect, because nature is prompt to decline, and if, in an Order so considerable you give any occasion of relaxation or any cause of trouble, you will most certainly be to blame before God. You are ill, it is true, but not so ill as not to be able to do without a soft bed, and not so weak as to make it necessary to nourish yourself with meat. It will happen that if at any time you do not grant the same dispensations to some Brothers, as ill, perhaps, and more so than yourself, the Brothers will fall into rash judgments and murmuring. This is why I exhort you to show yourself a good religious in these matters, as you have in other things. up till now." Then the pretended friend took leave of Jordan, muttering between his lips as if he were saying some of the Psalms.

The man of God had the simplicity to believe these words, and for several days abstained from all dispensations, until his feebleness increased so much that he could hardly walk about. Then it was revealed to him that the pretended friend of the Order was no other than the devil.

The old enemy even mocked Jordan with his

blindness. "Poor blind one," he said to him, "I wish to make some arrangement with thee. If thou consentest to preach no more, I promise not to tempt the souls of thy Friars any longer, and not to torment their bodies." But the holy man answered: "God forbid that I should contract an alliance with death, or that I should make any agreement with hell."

Father Gerard de Frachet devotes a long chapter to the wise answers of Blessed Jordan. They show a very admirable union of wisdom and religious spirit.

A Friar made great efforts to be released from the office of Procurator. The Master said to him: "Four things are usually attached to office—negligence, impatience, labor, and merit. I free you from the first two, but with regard to the others, I leave them to you for the expiation of your sins."

A Friar was accused in Chapter of having touched the hands of a woman. "But she was a pious woman," he said, to excuse himself. Jordan answered: "Water is good, earth is good, but mix them and you have mud."

God rewarded the virtues of his servant Jordan by giving him the power of frequently working miracles. In the Convent of Frankfort there was a Friar called Englebert, whom Blessed Jordan had received into the Order very young. But during the time of his novitiate he was attacked by a malignant fever. Jordan, seeing him feeble and dejected, said to him: "My son, if you have faith you can be quickly cured;" and the sick novice, having answered that he firmly believed, Master Jordan put his hands upon his head and said: "In the name of the Lord, return to health," and immediately he was freed from all traces of his fever.

The famous Father Thomas de Champre says that one day the Blessed was to preach in the presence of Pope Honorius, but at the time, when, according to monastic custom, he took a short sleep after dinner, a lay brother who had fallen into a weak state of mind, gave him a severe wound in the throat with a razor, as he lay asleep. The alarm was great in the convent, and sorrow was spread throughout the whole city. "What," cried the Pope, when he heard of it, "shall we lose this column of the Church?" Then one of the miracles which emanated from the man of God put an end to all anxiety. At the end of three days he rose from his bed, caused an altar to be got ready for him, and said Mass. When he came to the Communion he rubbed his throat with the second ablution, and his wound immediately closed.

During a journey in Thuringia he cured a woman of a disease of many years' standing, and, in the village of Aren, a priest given up by the doctors; another time, crossing the Alps, he gave the use of an eye to a smith who had lost it by the heat of the fire. But it would be an endless task to narrate all the marvels he worked.

Blessed Jordan had a most fervent devotion to St. Dominic; he wrote his life, and it was he who obtained the first solemn translation of his body. The holy founder of the Friar Preachers had been buried under a plain stone, in the Dominican Church at Bologna, where, day after day, a crowd of pilgrims knelt to pray before his humble shrine, and many miracles took place there.

But in the year 1223 the Fathers enlarged the convent, and it became necessary to remove the holy relics to another place. Gregory IX. readily granted permission for the translation, and deputed the Archbishop of Ravenna to represent him at the ceremony. It took place on the Tuesday of Whit week, May 24th, in the presence of the Archbishop, many Bishops, three hundred Dominican Fathers, who had assembled for the General Chapter, and a great number of priests and secular magnates.

When all stood around the tomb, and it had been opened, Blessed Jordan, with great reverence and devotion, took the body from the chest in which it lay, and placed it in a new one which was locked, and its key was given into the care of the civil authorities of the city. The chest was carried to a marble shrine and deposited there. A week afterwards, many who had not been present at the translation were allowed to see the holy body. Jordan unlocked the chest, and, taking the body into his arms, held it, while the Fathers and Brothers reverently and lovingly kissed it.

Blessed Jordan of Saxony.   65

Blessed Jordan wrote a letter to all the Priors of the Order, throughout the world, to announce this translation, and in July of the same year had the happiness of seeing his holy Father ranked among the saints of the Church and invoked upon her altars.

The servant of God had governed the Order for fifteen years, and after having presided over a General Chapter for the thirteenth time, in the year 1236, put into execution a pious design, which he had nourished in his mind a long time. It was to make a pilgrimage to the Holy Land, and at the same time to make a visitation in that newly founded province. The General Chapter of Paris, 1222, had established this province, and convents had already been built at Jerusalem, Damascus, Bethlehem, Nazareth, and in several other places of less note. His voyage out was happy, and in Palestine he satisfied his devotion in visiting that part of the earth which has been forever hallowed by the visible presence of the Word made flesh, Who deigned to dwell among us. He also labored much for the conversion of the infidels, and to improve the lax morals of the Christians who dwelt there.

In the beginning of the year following he started for home, and embarked on board ship with two Friars, Father Gerard, who had been his companion for eight years, and a lay Brother called John. There were in all ninety-nine persons on board. Hardly had the vessel put off from the coast when a terrible storm arose and they were soon wrecked. This was on the 13th of February, 1237. He, his two companions, and almost all the passengers perished. His body was thrown up by the sea upon the shore, and each night a shining light was seen hovering about it. This attracted the attention of some people, who went to see what it was. When they came near the holy body they smelt a perfume so delicious that those who lifted it up preserved it upon their hands for many days. The Dominicans of the town of Ptolymaide went to claim the body of their General, and buried it in their convent church.

Thus tragically ended the life of this lover of God, so full of zeal for His honor, and so fervent in laboring for the good of souls. His death was revealed to several holy religious, among whom was a Dominican Father at Limoges, supposed to be Father Gerard de Frachet, who gives an account of it in his book, and to St. Lutgard in Brabant. He appeared and consoled her when she was in a state of spiritual dryness, and told her that he was in heaven, and that she too would soon be called thither.

But the most beautiful apparition was that to a certain Carmelite Friar, who was preparing for death. He heard that blessed Jordan had been lost at sea, and was much troubled in his mind, for he said to himself, "is it, after all, vain to serve God? For was not this man who has perished a good man? Or is it that God does not reward those who serve him?" But that night a man, encircled with light, appeared to him in his sleep. Then, trembling and amazed he prayed: "Lord Jesus Christ, help me, and show me what this is." Then the vision said to him: "Be not alarmed, most dear Brother, I am Father Jordan of whom thou hast doubted. All who serve the Lord Jesus Christ shall be saved."

Then he disappeared, leaving the Father in great peace of soul. Many miracles took place by his intercession, so that he was always honored as a saint, even before he was included in the Dominican calendar. Pope Leo XII. solemnly approved his culture, May 10th, 1826, and allowed the whole Dominican Order to keep his feast.

Blessed Jordan was the author of several works. As well as the commentary on the gospel of St. Luke, before mentioned, he wrote a commentary on the Apocalypse, which is, however, attributed by some to another Jordan of Saxony, a hermit of St. Austin; several mathematical and grammatical works, many published sermons, a beautiful account of the commencement of the Dominican Order, and the life of St. Dominic. By some authors the Office of the feast of St. Dominic is attributed to him, but it would seem probable that it was written by a Dominican Bishop, Constantino, Bishop of Urbevetano.

But his greatest title to our gratitude is the great work to which he devoted all his talents and energies, the increase of the Order of Friar Preachers. When St. Dominic died there were eight provinces of the Order: Spain, France, Lombardy, Rome, Provence, Saxony, Hungary, and England, which, altogether, included sixty convents. To these Blessed Jordan added four others, Poland, Denmark, Greece and Palestine, each comprising many convents. He gave the habit to more than a thousand novices, among whom were St. Raymond of Pennafort; Blessed Gonzales; Blessed Albert the Great; Hugh of St. Cher, the first Dominican Cardinal; Blessed Humbert de Romanis; Cardinal Kilwarby, Archbishop of Canterbury; and Prince Garcia, son of the King of Navarre. In fine, he showed himself in every way a worthy successor to St. Dominic, which is the highest praise one can give him, and which it would have pleased him most to receive.

BLESSED ANTONY NEYROT.

BLESSED ANTONY NEYROT.

THERE is an endless variety in the lives of God's saints. In the calendar are to be found the names of kings and peasants, of strong men and feeble women, of those who have preserved the frail virtue of chastity unsullied in the very midst of most unfavorable circumstances, and of those who have hid themselves in monasteries or desert places, to keep their souls pure and undefiled. There are those who were all but sinless, and the fervent penitents, who, after years wasted in sin, touched by the grace of God, were led back again to Him, and expiated their sins in the fiery ways of penance. None, let his state be what it may, but can find an example and model among the saints of the Catholic Church, suited to his condition and state of life.

The saint whose life we now lay before our readers was of the class of penitents; and we know of few more instructive histories than that of his fall, glorious repentance, and generous atonement. It is indeed so forcible a lesson for us who have sinned, that it might almost be taken for a romance written with the express purpose of instruction.

In his youth Blessed Antony Neyrot gave himself to God, as we have done, but not with all his heart. There lurked within his soul a sad defect, which led him from little faults, by degrees, to renounce the faith of Jesus Christ, which alone could save him: just as we, alas! have so often sinned, in consequence of the fatal tendency to sin, which is the sad inheritance we have received from Adam, our common father, which we have been careless to repress and correct; and although we have not, like him, denied our Blessed Lord and His saving faith in express words, how often have not we done so in deeds, when we have stained our souls by some grievous sin!

Thus far the parallel between the life of

Blessed Antony and our spiritual life holds good ; let the perusal of this little history be an incentive to us to imitate him in his repentance, as we have so often resembled him in his fall, and although we may not be called upon, like him, to seal our conversion with our blood, we may, at least, learn a practical lesson of repentance for our sins, of generous resolve to amend, and of firmness in the midst of temptations.

A life of combat with our inclination to sin is scarcely less pleasing to God than the torments of martyrdom ; we may, therefore, gain a bright crown in Heaven, although we may not have the happiness, like Blessed Antony, to wash out the stains of sin with our life's blood. Let us, then, read the history of his life, not in the spirit of mere curiosity, but with reverence, so that we may, with simple hearts, learn a lesson from it.

Blessed Antony Neyrot was born at Rivoli, a small town in the neighborhood of Turin, in the beginning of the fifteenth century. We are told that he was of respectable family, but are left in ignorance of the exact date of his birth and of the details of his early life. We only know that he was very young when he entered the Order of St. Dominic, at Florence. The great St. Antoninus, who was Prior of the Convent of St. Mark at that time, clothed him with the habit, and gave him the religious name of Antony.

Having given satisfaction to his superiors in his novitiate, Blessed Antony was admitted to profession, and began his studies. He advanced quickly, and was more especially noted for his application to the study of the Holy Scriptures.

But the fatal defect in his natural character now began to appear. All the acts of his life, whether good or bad, show him to have been of a most ardent nature; and, if we may judge from the evident affection St. Antoninus had for him, giving him his own name, and from several other indications in the course of his life, he was possessed of very attractive qualities, which led all to love him. But he was young, infected with vanity, restless in mind, and desirous of change; he therefore asked his superiors to send him to another convent. St. Antoninus warned him that if he went it would be the cause of grievous misfortune to him. He was deaf to all advice, and was therefore sent by his superiors into Sicily. When he had been in that island sometime, he set out for Naples, and, as he was crossing the sea in a caracalla, a kind of Italian ship, he and all on board were taken captives by Nardo Anequino, a pirate, who, although a Christian, was nevertheless in the service of the Mahometan king of Tunis, in Africa, capturing Christians and selling them to him for slaves, in order to obtain a ransom for them from their families. This unfortunate event took place on the 2d of August, 1458. On the 10th of the same month he and his fellow captives were triumphantly led through the principal streets and squares of Tunis as a spectacle to the people, and then taken to prison.

There were many Christian captives in Tunis at that time, but considerable liberty was allowed them. Among them was a hermit of St. Jerome, Father Constantius of Cyprus. He heard that a young Dominican was in prison, and visited him at once, to console him in his trials, and to encourage him to persevere.

After the death of Blessed Antony, he wrote a letter to the Dominicans in Italy, giving an account of his imprisonment and of what afterwards befell him. He says that he found him in good dispositions in prison, except that he showed some signs of impatience under the heavy trials which had fallen upon him, for the Mahometans spared neither fair promises nor sufferings of all kinds in order to lead the captive Christians to apostatize and to embrace their odious doctrines.

Chains of iron round his ankles and wrists, frequent beatings, no food but stale bread and water, and a miserable bed for the night, caused his patience which had never been of the greatest, at length to give way. On condition that the imprisoned Christians took an oath not to escape, the king of Tunis occasionally allowed them to go out into the town. Unfortunately, Antony took advantage of this indulgence, and, instead of bearing his imprisonment as a trial sent him from God, lost no time in writing to the Genoese consul in Tunis to demand his ransom.

The consul was disedified at the tone of this

letter, for Antony had written with his usual impetuosity, and determined not to help him; but Father John, a Genoese Dominican, who was likewise in Tunis, probably a captive also, persuaded him to pay the ransom, and the consul did so from his own purse. Until instructions could be received from Genoa about the matter, Antony was kept in quasi-custody in the house of his brother Dominican.

But although he was to all intents and purposes quite free, allowed to wear the Dominican habit, and provided with all that was necessary, he still fretted under his trials; and, after six months spent in this way, when, indeed, he had but little excuse, he apostatized, and that publicly, in presence of a multitude of people, to the triumph of the Mahometans, but to the dismay and scandal of the Christians of Tunis. This was on the 6th of April, 1459. The miserable man even went so far as to sign his apostasy in his own blood, and was shortly after married to a Mahometan woman.

He occupied himself in translating parts of the Koran, the Mahometan sacred book, into

Italian; but seeing that it was nothing but a tissue of puerile absurdities, his eyes were opened, and he began to think of the fearful state he was in. Several Florentine merchants arrived at Tunis about the same time, bringing news of the death of St. Antoninus, who had clothed him with the Dominican habit, and who had always shown such affection for him. Antony soon heard of it and it touched his heart. Some authors say that the saint appeared to him in a vision, and reproached him for his apostasy. At any rate he repented of his grievous sin, and dismissed the woman he had called his wife, after having lived with her four months.

Abjuring the miserable superstition he had adopted, he began to pray once more to God, who had been so merciful to him, said the divine office regularly, and, by penance and prayer, nerved himself to the combat he saw must soon come. The King of Tunis was absent at the time, so Antony was forced to await his return for six months, wishing to renounce the Mahometan errors as publicly as he had embraced them. On Palm Sunday, April 16, 1460, the day on which the king was to return, Antony went to the little Catholic church, which was allowed for the use of the Christian merchants of Tunis; and having confessed to Father Constantius of Cyprus, and communicated, he said a few simple words to the Christians present, in which he lamented his apostasy, asked their pardon for the scandal he had given them, and declared that he was now ready to die for the Christian faith; and in proof of the sincerity of his repentance, was then reclothed in the Dominican habit by Father John, the Dominican, and, full of joy, went out to meet the king.

Then, in presence of all the crowd of Mahometans who had assembled, Antony, with loud voice, confessèd himself a Christian, renounced Mahometanism, and boldly declared himself ready to suffer for the love of Jesus Christ, his Saviour, and to prove the truth of his holy religion. The king, with that magnanimity which, in spite of all their faults, we must concede to the Mahometans, could not but admire his courage, and tried to shake his resolution. But Antony declared that he would never again deny his Redeemer and His divine religion. Whereupon the king, now angry, ordered him to be put in prison, unless he should at once apostatize. But Antony stood firm, and was accordingly taken back to prison. Three days' grace was given him, in hope that he would yet relent when brought so near death.

He was again very cruelly treated, and nothing was left untried to shake his resolution. On the fourth day, which was Holy Thursday, he was again taken before the king, to give his final answer, and happily, refused to abandon the true faith a second time. He was, therefore, condemned to be stoned to death.

Without delay he was led to the place of execution. When he had come to the spot, he asked for a few moments of prayer; which were granted him. He then took off his habit, and gave it to his executioners, telling them to keep it clean, as the Christians would gladly give them a large price for it. Then he knelt down, his face turned towards the east, and with hands stretched out in prayer, awaited the shower of stones which soon fell upon him. Not a word, not a murmur escaped him, although, as we have already said, he was of a most impatient nature. He knelt, unmoved, his eyes turned towards Heaven, until his soul, purified from its sins in the fiery trial of martyrdom, was freed from its prison house, and went to meet its Creator, against whom he had grievously sinned, but whom he had so gloriously confessed. Many Mahometans and Christians were witnesses of his death, and we are told that they all greatly admired his fervor and courage. His martyrdom took place on the 20th of March, 1460.

The bruised and bleeding remains of the martyr were thrown on a pile of wood to be burnt, but the flames respected them, and not a hair of his head was scorched. The executioners then carried the body through all the most frequented thoroughfares of the city, and cast it into the common sewer. Rescued from this vile place, at great cost, by the Genoese merchants, it was washed, and clothed in the Dominican habit by Father John, and then, in accordance with the martyr's own wishes, buried at the foot of a crucifix in the little Christian church at Tunis.

The humble grave of the martyr of Christ soon became a favorite place of prayer, and he was venerated by all as a saint. But four Christians, having received a miraculous cure through his intercession, it was thought prudent to send the holy relics to Genoa, for fear of the Mahometans. From Genoa they were again removed to Rivoli, his native place, in the year 1468, by Amadeus IX., Duke of Savoy, who was afterwards beatified. Many miracles took place both at Genoa and Rivoli, and a constant cultus having been proved, Clement X., on the 22d of February, 1767, approved it, and allowed the Dominican order to keep his feast each year on April 10.

The Dominican Fathers kept possession of his relics until they were driven out of their convent at Rivoli, at the end of the last century, by the Revolution. The convent buildings were afterwards turned into a school. But Blessed Antony is held in no less veneration in

Rivoli now than formerly, and his feast is kept every year, on the second Sunday after Easter, with great splendor and devotion. It is always preceded by a novena. On the day itself an immense gathering of the people, from all the neighboring towns and villages takes place, especially for the solemn procession in the afternoon after vespers, when a statue of the martyr is carried through all the streets of the town. All the religious confraternities, with their banners, and a great number of people carrying wax candles, take part in this procession. But the most interesting sight is the family of the saint, who number as many as a hundred, and who still live in the town, walking, clad in black, holding lighted tapers in their hands, following immediately after the statue of their holy kinsman. After the procession has re-entered the church, the ceremonies are ended by solemn benediction of the most holy sacrament, and when the people have satisfied their devotion towards the holy martyr by kissing his relics, they return to their homes.

BLESSED JAMES OF ULM.

BLESSED JAMES OF ULM.

THE Order of Preachers, which is justly famous for so many illustrious theologians and apostolic preachers who have united learning to sanctity, has been no less remarkable for the holiness of its more humble members, the lay brothers of the Order, who, although not learned in the things of this world, have yet been models of all religious virtues.

Amongst them, the Blessed James of Ulm holds a distinguished place. He was born in the year 1407, at Ulm, a wealthy city in the South of Germany. He was the second son of Theodore, a merchant of that town, who was very pious and noted for his charity to the poor. He lived to an honorable old age, "without losing," as Blessed James loved to say, "a single tooth from his head," on account of his abstinence and regularity of his life.

James was educated piously, and in his youth was employed in mechanical arts, but more especially in that of making stained glass windows, for which his countrymen have long been famous. He remained in the bosom of his family until he was twenty-five years old, when the desire to visit the tombs of the holy Apostles Peter and Paul determined him to undertake a journey to Rome. On setting out he knelt down and asked the blessing of his beloved father, who gave it to him in these words, "Go, my son, call your Creator to mind during the whole of the road, and choose rather to die than sin in His sight. When you are at the holy places think of me, an old man who begot you. Return as soon as possible, for you are my joy, my crown, and the staff of my old age. May the merciful Creator bless you, my dearest son, and make you a partaker of His eternal happiness." . This beautiful exhortation was not made in vain, for when he and some companions, who were also bound for the Eternal City, began their journey, James said to them, "Let each of us my friends, search his conscience lest this journey be spoilt by any sin, that we may with a clear conscience gain the indulgences granted to pilgrims;" and the whole of the time they were on the road he kept himself always occupied with some holy work, praying or meditating, sometimes saying verses out of the psalms, sometimes reciting the Lord's prayer.

They arrived in Rome about the beginning of Lent. He spent the penitential season in visiting the churches, and prepared himself to celebrate the feast of Easter by a general confession of his whole life. When Easter was over, having come to the bottom of his purse, he went to Naples to seek some means of subsistence. Being well-made and handsome, a noble lady of that town, who had many servants, having seen him, wished to take him into her service, but the virtuous young man, fearing some danger for his soul, declined, choosing poverty rather than put himself wilfully in the occasions of sin.

At last he was forced by hunger and want to enlist as a soldier in the army of Alphonsus II., King of Naples. In this new state of life, living among men not usually noted for strictness of morals, his virtues shone forth very brightly. He was pious, modest, chaste, and what was almost unknown among soldiers, content with his pay. His horror of the sin of theft, so common among soldiers, was very great, and was the cause of his leaving the army. He lodged with some of his comrades in the house of a Jew, and having arrived too late one day for dinner, one of them gave him the remains of a plate of vegetables, saying that they had been stolen. He put it away from him indignantly, and on the morrow sought and obtained his dismissal.

From Naples he went to Capua, and entered the service of a nobleman who soon learnt to appreciate him and to love him. He gave him his whole confidence, and treated him rather as a son than as his servant. James remained five years in this capacity, but desiring to see his father once more, set out to return to his own country.

Passing through Bologna, he went to the church of the Friar Preachers, where lies the body of Saint Dominic, and was so edified by the holy and mortified life of the Dominicans, that, sacrificing the love of his native land, and giving up all hope of ever seeing his aged father again, he asked to be received among them as a lay brother. His desire was granted, and he received the habit from the Prior of the convent, Father Nicholas Carbonelli, and began his noviciate. This was in the year 1438, when he was 31 years of age.

He again took up glass painting which he had given up when he had left his father's house in Ulm, and was given the task of filling the windows of the Dominican church and monastery at Bologna. They were so beautiful that they made him famous; unhappily they have all perished, and nothing remains of his work in the church or monastery, except a small medallion at the entrance to the dormitories of the monastery. It represents our blessed Lord hanging on the cross. The windows he made for the great Basilica of Saint Petronio, and a little chapel of Saint Helen in the Bentivoglio palace in Bologna still remain entire, and they are quite worthy of the praise contemporary authors bestow on them. To him is ascribed the discovery of a beautiful transparent yellow tint, by means of oxyde of silver.

While he was thus turning his talents to the service of God, he did not neglect his spiritual advancement. He had a very ardent desire to serve his Creator, and going one day, soon after he was clothed in the Dominican habit, to the novice master, he said, "Dear Father, having left the world and having received this habit, I wish to serve my God more fervently; therefore, with all my heart I beseech you to show me the way, and to instruct me how I may arrive at the heavenly kingdom."

"My dear son," answered the holy novice master, "There are two cities, to either of which every man must go. The first is called Babylon, which means 'Confusion.' It is a furnace of raging fire, in which all those who die in mortal sin are punished. In it the proud, the unchaste, the self-willed, the rebellious, and the disobedient, are damned forever. The road which leads to this city is pride, the mother and begetter of all vices. Satan, who is the king of all the sons of pride, dwells in this city.

"The other city, dear son, is that which is above, the city of Jerusalem, which means 'a vision of peace.' In this city dwell all blessed souls and saints, ever most joyfully praising the power of God the Father, the manhood of God the Son, and the wisdom and goodness of God the Holy Ghost. The King of this city is our Lord Jesus Christ, who is King of Kings, and Lord of Lords. The road to it is holy humility, which is the guardian and preserver of all virtues; as says St. Gregory, 'He who gathers together all virtues without humility, is like him who carries dust in his hands during a storm.'

"In order that you may embrace this holy virtue, the Saviour, Jesus Christ Himself, invites you by his own example, saying, 'Learn of Me, because I am meek and humble of heart.' The most blessed Mother of God, our Advocate, also praises it in these words, 'He hath regarded the humility of his handmaid.'

"There are then two ways, one called 'Humility,' which leads to the heavenly city; the other, called 'Pride,' which leads to everlasting fire. Choose the one which pleases you best, dear son; yet I exhort you to enter the path of humility, that you may be raised to honor hereafter."

These beautiful words produced the desired effect in his heart. "Blessed be God in His gifts," he said; "I choose the way of humility, and with my whole heart I will follow it." Nor were these mere idle words; he at once set about to cultivate this holy virtue in his heart, so that humility became his most striking virtue. He thought himself the inferior of all men, and became in very deed and truth the servant of all.

A few days after his entrance into religion some of his old companions and fellow pilgrims from Germany to Rome, who were then at Bologna, went to see him at the convent, accompanied by the commandant of the citadel, by whom Blessed James had formerly been employed. This man, turning to the Fathers who were present, said, "Very reverend Fathers, this young man, whom you have received into your Order, is the most modest and most virtuous man I have ever seen; none of us have ever known him to do or say the least thing deserving of blame, and as for us, we have never dared to say a single useless word in his presence. I am sorry, not that he has joined you, but to be deprived of a young man so pious and so modest."

So great, indeed, was the opinion the Fathers themselves formed of his holiness that they awaited the time for his profession with much impatience, for they feared, although there was no ground for fear, lest they should lose him. When the time came he made a general confession, and pronounced his vows with great fervor.

His life after his profession grew more and more saintly. Instead of growing colder in the love of God, as is too often the case, he increased his austerities and penances, and his heart drew nearer and nearer to God. We shall best gain some idea of his virtues and conduct by describing his daily life.

He was always first in the choir in the morning, and hidden in some out-of-the-way chapel, said the prayers which the rule prescribes for lay-brothers. Then he visited all the altars in the church, always beginning with the altar of our Lady, to whom he had a most tender devotion. When it was the day to communicate, after having spent the day before in profound silence and recollection of soul, he meditated through the long hours of the night, and early in the morning confessed his sins, "or what his utter whiteness held for sin," and then went to the altar to receive his Lord and Master from the hands of the priest. Then he fell into a profound peace of mind, and seemed as if in an ecstasy the whole of the day.

He had a great devotion to the Passion of our blessed Redeemer, and day by day meditated it in his heart. He imagined, first of all, that he saw our Lord washing the feet of His disciples at the last supper; then he called to mind the agony in the garden, and so on, until he came to the sad end on Calvary, and the entombment of the sacred body of his Lord. Then he meditated on the five glorious mysteries of the Holy Rosary, and when he had placed his risen Lord upon His eternal throne in heaven, and seen His holy Mother crowned Queen of the heavenly kingdom, he made a profound reverence before the Lamb of God, upon the mystic altar in heaven, and said, "Glory be to Thee, O Lord, and glory be to the Father, and to the Holy Ghost. Thou, O Lord, who wast born of the Virgin Mary, befriend me this day and forever." Then turning to the Mother of God, whom he also saluted reverently he said, " Hail O Queen of Heaven ; Hail Mother of the King of the Apostles ; Hail Mary flower of Virgins, beautiful as the rose, chaste as the lily ! pray thou to thy Son for me, and for all people." Then he turned to the choir of saints and said to them, "O all ye Saints of God, intercede for my salvation, and for the salvation of the whole world."

When this holy and simple man had thus ended his prayer he betook himself to his daily work, in which he never seemed to feel any fatigue, for his desire to merit in the sight of

God was so great that he never thought of the wants and needs of his body In the evening, when it came to the time for retiring to rest, he carefully examined all the acts of the day and his conversation, made a fervent act of contrition, and took a severe discipline; then he lay down to rest, and thus ended the day.

Blessed James wore an iron chain round his waist, and practised many other severe mortifications, yet he was not at all reserved or severe in his manner; he was always serene and joyful, always gentle and cheerful, and ever ready to do a good turn to any one. He was also very careful to guard against any singularity, and loved all the common duties of religious life. He ate the same food and in the same quantity as the others, knowing well that an affectation of mortification is often the first step to pride and self-righteousness.

He practised the three virtues of poverty, obedience, and chastity in great perfection. He was always content when he had the bare necessaries of life, and loved to say that he not only possessed nothing of his own, but that he was himself the property of Another. When it was time to go to the refectory he would often say to the other lay brothers, " Let us go, my dearest brothers, and see if the fathers will give us something to eat."

His spirit of obedience was very great, and although he practised all other virtues in great perfection, yet obedience seems to have been his characteristic virtue. Obedience is in truth the outward manifestation of humility, or, in other words, it is humility put into practice.

When his superiors told him to do anything he began at once, without the slightest delay, almost before the words had passed their lips. Many beautiful anecdotes of his obedience are to be found in his life, written by Fra Ambrogio Soncino. We will select one or two which give us the best idea of its perfection.

One day, when Father Michael of Holland was Prior of Bologna, a certain Bishop went to see the convent, and it happened that as he was walking through the cloisters with the Prior, blessed James passed by them. The Prior said to the Bishop, "Right reverend Father, he who passed us just now is a very devout Brother, very religious, and a true servant of God." "Yes," replied the Bishop, "his venerable looks told me that." Then said the Prior, "he is the most obedient Brother in the convent, and if it please you, I should like to prove it to you." "Most gladly," answered the Bishop. Then they went together to a room where blessed James was at work, most likely engaged in glass staining, and the Prior said to him, "Brother James, you must go and take some letters to the most reverend Father-General, who is at Paris." Blessed James at once prepared to set out, and asked the Prior's blessing, customary for travellers, making no other preparations than to beg leave to go to his cell to find his staff. But the Prior appearing to have suddenly changed his mind, told him that he need not go, and blessed James returned to his work without further delay.

A certain citizen of Bologna invited the Dominicans to pass a day with him in the country, kindly thinking that the pure, fresh air would do them much good, and would recreate them. Blessed James went with the rest. But when all the others had dined, the head of the brothers said to him, "Brother James, go quickly with the brothers to fish, that we may have something for supper." He went at once, although he had had nothing to eat, and cast his net in the river Reno, which was at a little distance. The first time he caught so many fish that two friars could hardly carry them, and yet the net was not broken. Thus his prompt obedience was rewarded by God, who repays a hundredfold all that his creatures do for love of him.

But the most beautiful anecdote is the following. He was busy one day staining some glass, and had just put it into the furnace to burn when a brother came to him and said, "Father Prior wishes you to go with me to beg some bread in the town." Now blessed James knew well that if he left his work at that moment it would be entirely spoilt, and the labor of whole days would be thrown away : yet he hesitated not an instant, and went at once into the city with the brother leaving the glass to its fate. But God rewarded his obedience. When he returned he found that the glass, far from being ruined, was so beautiful that he had never before done anything like it, "He so loved this virtue of obedience," says Fra Ambrogio, "that he thought the day lost if he had not exercised it."

His charity for his neighbor showed itself in a thousand beautiful ways, but more especially in his care for the sick. As soon as he heard that any of the community was ill, he would hasten to ask the Prior's leave to nurse him. When he came to the infirmary he would wait upon the sick brother with joyful heart, and cheer him with merry words, while he got ready all which was necessary for him. Many of the brothers firmly believed that they were cured not by the medicines which they took, but by the merits of the humble lay brother, who served them with such holy care. "My dear brothers," he once said, when speaking of charity, "labor to acquire this virtue, for it is the wedding garment without which no one can enter the heavenly feast, and they who have it not are cast forth into the outer darkness where is weeping and gnashing of teeth."

He never soiled himself by any sin against purity, but served God with a pure mind and with a chaste soul. He made use of two means for this end; the first was to keep a constant and steady guard over his eyes, knowing well that they are often the cause of sin : and the other was to force his body to labor always. By these two means, united to his prayers and other mortifications, he kept down all unruly motions, so that he lived the life of an angel upon earth. He often exhorted the brothers to be very careful to preserve this fragile virtue, and was heard to say that no temptation of the flesh is so strong that it cannot be overcome by the sweet name of Jesus, or by meditating on the Passion of our Blessed Redeemer.

Miracles were not wanting as an evidence of his holiness. He cured a certain priest of Bologna, who was dangerously ill, by merely passing his hand from the head to the feet of the sick man, when he was immediately restored to health. This priest, who was a very good artist, painted a picture of the saint, which he put on his tomb after his death.

There was a German student at Bologna, who had suffered from violent headache for four months, so that he began to debate in his mind whether he should not give up his studies and return to his native land. But one day a certain man asked him why he seemed to be so sad, and when he heard the reason, said to him, "Go to St. Dominic's, and ask for Brother James, who by his prayers will cure you." The poor youth went, and when he found his saintly countryman, humbly asked him to cure him. The saint at first declined, saying that he was but a poor sinner. But the student remained at the convent door, weeping and imploring him to put his hands upon his head, and he would be quite satisfied. Blessed James was obliged to give way, and placing his hands upon the student's head, said, " May God, who created thee, heal thee," and immediately the youth was cured.

Blessed James was often wrapt in ecstacies, and we have an account of one of them from his own lips: "He once said to me," says Fra

Ambrogio, "when we were at work together, alone, 'When I was in one of the cells I was so strongly seized with a desire to pray that—how I know not, God only knows—I was withdrawn from my bodily senses. My soul was carried into a beautiful meadow, full of all delights, where fragrant roses and the sweetest violets grew in the grass; and my soul was so content with this sweetness that I wished to have stayed there forever; but, unhappily, a brother passing by found me, and thinking I was dead quickly called the Prior; then all the fathers and brothers ran together, and by dint of violent rubbing brought me round. And when I saw so many brothers in my presence, I said, 'I warrant you, dear brothers, that no greater misfortune could have befallen me, for you have disturbed my soul rejoicing in such consolation.'"

He was often seen encircled with heavenly light, and when Fra Ambrogio, to whom he told the secrets of his heart, questioned him about it, he said that it was so bright in the middle of the night that he could distinctly see the smallest objects. This eminent holiness displeased the enemy of souls, and we need not therefore be surprised to read that he was greatly annoyed by horrible apparitions. Thus one day, as he was praying in the chapel of Saint Vincent, a demon, ugly as sin, appeared to him. No Ethiopian could have been blacker, and, to increase his ugliness, he had only one eye, which was placed in the middle of his forehead; but Blessed James made the all-powerful sign of the cross, and the unclean imp of Satan vanished.

The reputation he had acquired in Bologna spread abroad, and he was well known as a saint far and near. Many persons went to Bologna to see him, and to recommend themselves to his prayers. Among them was the Duke of Calabria, afterwards Alphonsus II., King of Sicily, who, being in the town, went to visit him. He embraced him, and humbly recommended himself to his prayers. When Blessed James had retired, the Duke expressed himself in terms which showed how much he had been impressed by him, and what a high opinion he had formed of his sanctity.

Towards the end of his life, he was attacked by the infirmities which are the almost inseparable companions of old age, but he knew how to bear them with resignation. He not only suffered them without murmuring, but even with joy, repeating often those words of the Apostle, "Strength is made perfect in weakness. Gladly, therefore, will I glory in my infirmities." (2 Cor. xii. 9.)

He was eighty-four years of age when he was seized with a violent fever, which brought him to the grave. He received the last sacraments, placed himself in the form of a cross, and died. This was on the 12th of October, in the year 1491. He was laid in the same tomb in which Saint Dominic had first been buried, in the presence of an immense multitude of people, who reverenced him as a saint. But eight days after, owing to the great numbers who came to pray at his tomb, it became absolutely necessary to translate the holy body into a place more easy of access, and it was accordingly taken to the chapel in which reposes the body of Saint Dominic, where it now lies.

Many miracles took place at his tomb, among which one claims our attention. Brother Denis of Beccano, at that time a student in the convent at Bologna, was ill of a grave malady, so that he could not attend any of the services in the choir. When the holy lay brother was on his death-bed he asked him to pray for him as soon as he should be admitted into the presence of God, that he might be freed from his illness, and be able to fulfill the duties of his state. When the saint lay dead this poor novice went to the cell in which the body lay, and throwing himself upon it, ceased not to call upon Blessed James in these words :—" Fulfill, O Saint, what thou hast promised, and cure me by thy prayers," and could not be pulled away from the body until he had obtained his desire, and was freed from his complaint.

This, and many other miracles, caused a great devotion to him to spring up among the people, which has continued down to our times; but it was not until the year 1825 that it was solemnly approved by the Church. Leo XII., July 30th, 1825, granted permission to the

Dominican Order, and to the diocese of Bologna, to keep his feast on October 12th.

His life was written as we have already said, by Fra Ambrogio Soncino, who was his pupil in the art of glass staining, and was constantly with him. He wrote it in Italian, but it was afterwards translated into Latin by another Dominican, Father Isidore of Milan.

BLESSED GILES OF SANTAREM.

BLESSED GILES OF SANTAREM.

CHAPTER I.

TOWARDS the end of the twelfth century there lived at the court of Sancho, King of Portugal, a nobleman of the highest rank, Councillor of the King, and Governor of Coimbra, called Don Roderigo Paez. His first wife having died, he had married Dona Teresa Gilea, a lady of rank equal to his own. By her he had several children, Blessed Giles being his third son. He was born at his father's castle of Vaozela, between Coimbra and Viseau. The date of his birth is uncertain, but it seems to have been about the year 1190. He was christened Giles Roderigo, after both his mother and father. He had four brothers, one of whom became an ecclesiastic, like himself.

He was destined by his parents to the ecclesiastical state from his youth, according to the custom of those times, and was piously educated for this end. When he had arrived at a sufficient age he was sent to study at the University of Coimbra. Although he was still young and not yet ordained, his father's influence gained for him several rich benefices, such as two monasteries, and three canonries, in the cathedrals of Braga, Coimbra, and Idanha. But the wealth he was thus possessed of was a great evil to him, for instead of studying to acquire a stock of learning suited to his future life as an ecclesiastic, he thought only of making a name for himself in the world, and how to pass for a man of wit and education. And, alas! his rank and riches were the ruin of his innocence, for he fell into habits of deadly sin, and spent all the time he did not give to study, in the pursuit of sinful and hollow pleasures. He especially studied medicine, and being naturally of good parts, became so proficient in that science that he soon gained the reputation of knowing the deepest secrets of nature.

In this depth of spiritual and moral degradation, he received sacred orders, but did not change his life; he remained no less worldly and ambitious as a priest than he had been as a layman. The study of the Holy Scriptures and Theology, to which, by reason of his state, he ought to have given himself, was neglected and despised by him, and he spent all his time and talents in acquiring a reputation as a learned and successful physician.

But although the young priest was a scandal to all pious people, God had not abandoned him, and brought him under the influence of saintly and mortified men, who charmed him by their holiness and austerities from his evil life into the ways of penance and peace. Desirous to perfect his already extensive knowledge of medicine, he left Coimbra to study at the famous University of Paris. He soon gained the same reputation there as in his native country, and was rewarded by a doctor's degree. Dazzled by the honors showered upon him, he now thought he had arrived at the goal of his desires, but God had other designs for him.

He came in contact with the Dominican Fathers, and the sweet odor of their holy and mortified lives converted him back to his God, whom he had forgotten so long, and against whom he had so often and so grievously sinned. Some authors say that he was among the numerous conquests made by the eloquence of Blessed Jordan of Saxony, who was drawing so many fervent souls into the ranks of the Friars of Mary at that time. It is certain that he was in the noviciate of St. James, at Paris, with Blessed Humbert de Romanis; he must, therefore, have received the habit of St. Dominic either in the year 1224 or 1225.

This is all that is certain about his conversion and entrance into the Dominican Order, but some Spanish authors say that as he was traveling from Coimbra to Paris, the devil in human form accosted him, and having entered into conversation with him, persuaded him to deny God, and to enter into his service, promising him that he should become so able in medicine as to outstrip the most celebrated doctors of Paris. Giles, according to this romantic history, passed so long a time as seven years in a cave near Toledo, learning the secrets of nature from his infernal master; although one would have thought that the devil could have taught them in a much shorter time. In return for the knowledge thus laboriously acquired, these authors say that he opened a vein in his arm, and signed a deed in his own blood transferring his soul to the devil.

He then went to Paris, where he, in truth, acquired a great reputation. But one night as he was studying in his room a frightful spectre entered, and in a fearful voice threatened to kill him if he did not change his life. This alarming vision was repeated three times. Blessed Giles was converted, and set out to return to Portugal, but coming to Palencia, found some of the first disciples of St. Dominic, just arrived there, and engaged in building a monastery with their own hands. He at once made up his mind to join them, and after confessing his sins was clothed in the Dominican habit by the Prior. He divided his goods among his servants, and sent them back to Portugal with a letter to his father stating what he had done.

This history continues thus: After spending

seven years in rigid penance, to expiate his seven years of servitude to the devil, he was rewarded by God by receiving possession of the fatal document in which he had sold his soul, and which he at once destroyed.

This history is supported by no sufficient authority. The famous book called the " Vitæ Fratrum," which was written by the order and under the supervision of Blessed Humbert de Romanis, who, as we have said, was a fellow novice of Blessed Giles, although it speaks of his sinful youth and of his sudden conversion to God, says nothing about it, nor do any authors until the sixteenth century. We may, therefore, doubt its truth without incurring any suspicion of being hypercritical.

There is another but more poetical form of the same history. After narrating how he passed seven years in the cave at Toledo, and his wonderful success and reputation at Paris, it continues thus: One night he fell asleep, tired out with his labors of the day, and while he slept it seemed as if he were transported to one of the Portuguese monasteries, of which he enjoyed the revenues. It was night, but the moon shone brightly, and everything was distinctly visible. Suddenly the bell in the tower rang out with startling effect in the midnight air. Before the last solemn sound had died away he saw a grave open, and a fearful spectre glide out, clad in a shroud. The horrible skeleton held a skull in one hand and an hour-glass in the other.

It passed along amid the silent tombs, but suddenly stopped before one of them, and cried out in a hollow voice: "Arise, unfaithful monk; thou who didst break thy vows, arise!" and Blessed Giles saw another spectre, of a dead monk, come forth from its resting place, and follow him who called it. After a little while it stopped again, and cried out as before, "Faithless monk, arise!" and a second arose and followed him. Thus the fearful spectre went through the whole cemetery, and called the souls of those who had been sinful religious to join the horrible procession.

At last he came to a tomb where, to the inexpressible horror of Blessed Giles, he cried out,

"Giles, thou who hast broken thy vows, arise!" But no sound or movement came from the tomb. "Where is he, then?" said the spectre. He looked at his hour-glass; there were yet a few grains of sand to run. "Giles," he said, "thy hour has not yet come, but it will not be long."

Then the spectres, dropping their shrouds, began an infernal dance upon the graves. Suddenly they all stopped, rushed at him, and their chief cried out, "Miserable wretch, evil be to thee if thou dost not change thy life;" and the spectral chorus rang in his ears, "Change thy life." Then their chief thrust him through the heart with his sickle, but Giles, who had always kept some remnant of love and devotion to Mary in his heart, called upon her holy name, and the ghastly vision vanished.

Although we are forced to say that these poetical accounts of his conversion are devoid of historical proof, yet they may be taken as evidence of the marvelous reputation Blessed Giles had acquired, and they also verify the suddenness of his conversion to God and change of life. His was not one of those half conversions which are so common, when the soul turns towards God indeed, but never loses its longing for its former sins, and in consequence frequently falls into what it professes to have abandoned. Blessed Giles, on the contrary, became a new man. He had led a life of sinful indulgence; he had drunk of the intoxicating cup of unlawful pleasure; but at the voice of God he broke through his former habits of sin, and became in very truth a true model of a fervent penitent. The gay, licentious student became a modest Friar, the self-indulgent youth a poor religious, who walked in the ways of holy obedience and penance, and fought with energy and success against the evil inclinations of corrupt nature, which had gained so strong a hold upon him owing to the years he had spent in habits of sin.

The seed of the Word had fallen on ground long untilled indeed, but fertile, which, watered by the grace of God, produced a harvest of beautiful Christian virtues, in the place of the noxious weeds of impurity and pride, which so recently had grown there. The severe austerities laid down by the Dominican rule were hardly enough to satisfy his ardent desire of penance. He never forgot that he had spent many years in sinful pleasures, and knew that, although God in his mercy had forgiven him the guilt of his sins, still there was yet the temporal debt due to his justice to pay. He wore a hair shirt, carried an iron belt round his body, and if obedience had not forbidden, would have set no bounds to his disciplines and other bodily mortifications.

CHAPTER II.

BLESSED GILES was naturally witty in conversation, very gay and charming in manner. This had no doubt been to him an occasion of sin, and the cause of his loving gay society. So it happened that when he entered the Dominican Order he found it very difficult to keep the strict silence enjoined by the rule, and to refrain from idle words. He so fretted at first under this mortification that he could hardly contain himself; it even seemed as if a hot fire burnt his breast and throat when he attempted to keep the silence. But one day, illumined by the Holy Spirit, he saw that this was a temptation of the evil one, and made a resolution that he would remain in his place and keep silence in the common recreation, although he should be burnt up with the fire in his throat, and thus, quaintly says the old writer, "be obliged to make a noise." Then God, seeing his courage and firmness, took this temptation from him, and made silence so delicious to his soul that he became truly remarkable for his spirit of constant recollection and guard over his tongue.

Blessed Humbert de Romanis, his fellow novice, says of him that he never knew him to say an idle word, but when he spoke it was either to console the desolate and sad in spirit, or to speak of holy things. He also adds that Blessed Giles was so desirous of hiding his talents, that although he was a famous physician, he always took the remedies prescribed him in sickness by his superiors, even when he knew that they were by no means the best for him.

He thought himself the most wicked in the convent, and could hardly debase himself enough to punish his former pride and sin. He was full of charity towards his brothers, especially to those who were ill. When the students went to class, this humble penitent made the round of their cells, and did all the little services necessary for the comfort of their inmates; a small thing to do, no doubt, but one which vividly shows us the goodness and humility of his heart.

By the practice of severe self-repression his soul was purified from its natural tendency to luxury and ease, and he felt a sweet peace which more than repaid him for all his mortifications. Oh! if the world knew the joy which God pours into the hearts of those who give up all for him in the monastic life, what crowded monasteries of fervent religious should we not see in this our own land! But all is not easy in the battle against self, and Blessed Giles found this to be the case. God, to try him, and to ground him well in humility, and to fix his heart upon his Creator alone, withdrew all sensible sweetness from his soul, and at the same time the devil whispered in his ear that he had embraced a life far above his strength of body and soul. But Blessed Giles vanquished this temptation by prayer, and was freed from the temptation. One day, being very violently tried, he went to his confessor, and told him all about it. "Dearest Brother," said the Father to him, "remember that you led a soft and luxurious life in the world, and therefore receive this trial not only with patience, but even gladly, as a penance and satisfaction for your sins, for the Lord is with thee." God was pleased with the humility which had caused Blessed Giles to manifest this temptation to his confessor, and gave such power to the Father's words that it at once left him never to return.

In due time Blessed Giles made his religious profession, and began to study theology, which in his pride he had neglected and despised when a student at Coimbra. In this beautiful science he made great progress, as might have been expected, not only on account of his great natural abilities, but also on account of his holiness and purity of intention, for he now studied with the sole end of knowing God and to fit himself to labor for the salvation of souls. He especially delighted in the study of Holy Scripture. He gained the grade of Lector, or professor, in philosophy and theology at the end of his course of studies.

After several years spent in the monastery of St. James at Paris, his superiors seeing of what use he would be for the salvation of souls in his own country and among his own people, sent him back to Portugal, where his relations and the Dominican fathers had long been awaiting him. So he returned to the scenes of his youth. But how changed from what he had been a few short years before when he had scandalized all pious souls by his licentious life! He had left Coimbra for Paris a thorough worldling, full of proud and impure thoughts, intent only upon himself and forgetful of his Maker; he returned a beautiful example of the mercy of God, a holy and fervent disciple of the Crucified, a true penitent, and burning with zeal for the honor and glory of God. Then, robed in the richest this world could afford, surrounded by luxuries and softness; now a poor friar, with nothing he could call his own, clad in a coarse white habit, the tonsure-crown of thorns upon his head, suffering fatigue and hunger, striving to make his whole life a cross in reparation for those sins which he had committed in his youth. In the eyes of the world he had lost all which it prizes; in the sight of God he had gained everything.

The chronology of Blessed Giles' life is difficult to unravel, but it is probable that he left Paris in the year 1229. One of the first disciples of Saint Dominic, Suere Gomez, was provincial of Spain and Portugal at that time. He received Blessed Giles with open arms, and with that loving heart which saints alone possess. He sent him to the convent of Lisbon to teach theology and to preach. He also charged him at various times with the difficult task of founding new monasteries. His virtues shone very brightly in the monastery of Lisbon. He never offended any one, but was gentle and charitable towards all. He was always occupied either in prayer, reading, study, or meditation. Above all things he loved to read the lives of the saints and fathers of the Church. He had an ardent affection for his own order, and by every means in his power encouraged it in others. He constantly exhorted his fellow religious to study to acquire the virtue of holy purity in its perfection, and no less insisted upon the absolute necessity of a spirit of true obedience. He was gifted with a special power to console the tempted and desolate; none ever went away from him unconsoled. He nursed the sick with his own hands, and often told them that he no longer put his hopes in medicine, but in the power of God; "for," he said, "grace can do more than the doctor." When anyone spoke of mere worldly things he kept silence, until with holy and prudent tact, he could gradually lead back the conversation to God, or to some saintly subject. He could never hear an idle word, and is said never to have spoken about himself during his life in holy religion.

He was often wrapped in holy ecstacies when he meditated, and was so carried out of himself that he did not know when anyone entered his cell or sat down at his side; but when he came to himself he would rise at once to welcome him, as if he had just come in.

The King of Portugal wishing to have the children of St. Dominic in the town of Santarem, Blessed Giles was sent by his superiors to build a new monastery there. He preached in that town with wonderful success, and led many strayed souls back to the friendship of God. But here, as elsewhere, his presence, breathing an atmosphere of mortification and severe self-repression, did more for the conversion of souls than his words, although they alone were enough to move the hardest hearts.

While at Santarem he became the firm friend and confessor of the two infantas, Sancha and Teresa. They no sooner saw him than they formed a very high opinion of his holiness, and chose him for their confessor and confidential adviser, and loved to speak with him of God. The infanta Sancha especially venerated him, and always fell on her knees to ask his blessing, and beg the help of his prayers. "Pray for me," she would say, "give me your blessing and pray for me. She entered the Cistercian Order, and died, with the reputation of holiness, in the year 1229. One night, after her death, she appeared to the saint as he lay half asleep in his cell. He was much disturbed, fearing some diabolical illusion, but when he saw who it was, he said, "Is it well with you, Sancha?" She answered, "It is well with me, owing to the grace of God and your prayers. Peace be to you;" and she vanished. And such force, says his biographer, had this virginal visit, that from that time he never felt any unruly motions of the flesh, nor was troubled in his mind by any involuntary unlawful thoughts. Blessed Giles told this beautiful visit to a certain Father Bartholomew, who revealed it after the death of the saint.

Blessed Giles preached in most of the cities and towns of Portugal, but with most especial success at Coimbra, the scene of the follies and sins of his youth. As a student he had been the scandal of the town, but on his return, by the grace of God, he made glorious amends for all the evil he had caused there in his youthful days. He returned to preach the hollowness of all human delight, and his sermons converted many souls. It must have been a continual source of humiliation to the humble servant of God to live in this town, for every street must have called to his mind the sins and excesses of his youth; but he was sent there by his superiors, and his simple obedience was amply rewarded by God.

The reputation Blessed Giles had gained by

this time, and his success as a preacher of the Word of God and the founder of new monasteries, caused the Fathers of the Spanish Province to elect him Provincial in the year 1234, at the death of Suere Gomez, the first Provincial. The votes of the electors were unanimous. He was much affected, but accepted the office from motives of purest obedience to the wishes of his fellow religious. Always at the beck of his superiors, and ever ready to work for the good of souls and the increase of the Dominican Order, he simply did what he was asked to do, although to be in authority was very distasteful to him.

He at once set to work, and visited all the monasteries of the province, and in every respect fulfilled the expectations formed of him. But he did not let his new duties hinder him from preaching, nor did he, in the slightest, mitigate his penances and austerities. While in office he went to assist at several general chapters of the Order in France, Germany, and Italy.

CHAPTER III.

AMONG the incidents recorded of the life of Blessed Giles there is one which in all probability took place on his return from the Chapter at Paris. On his way back to Portugal he traveled one day without having anything to eat for many hours, and being very weak on account of his long fasts, became excessively tired. So he proposed to his companion that they should turn aside to the nearest village to get something to eat, but the Father, who was strong and vigorous, thought it better to go on until they came to some larger village or town, where they would be more likely to get what they needed. While they thus stood talking in the middle of the road a noble dame, accompanied by a large train of servants, came up. She loved the Fathers of the Dominican Order very much, and was much pleased to see them. She at once saw from his sanctified appearance that Blessed Giles was a very holy man, and turning to her son, a stripling at her side, said, "Peter my child, for the fear of God and the love of man, provide everything necessary for these holy men, who are tired with their journey."

The youth went at once to carry out his mother's behest, and having led the Fathers to her castle, and prepared a room for them to take a little rest, set a strengthening repast before them, consisting of a good fish pie, says the old author, which his mother had made herself, wine, eggs, new bread, and cheese. This pious and obedient youth not only waited upon the Fathers at their meal, but filled up their cups with wine, and helped them to the dishes so cheerfully, inviting them to eat and drink so charmingly, that he won the saint's heart, who, pleased to see such politeness and care for the poor of Christ in a child so young, said to his companion when they had returned thanks to God for the dinner He had given them, "Let us pray to the blessed Lord and to the most clement Virgin to watch over and to choose for themselves this youth, who has waited upon us so well," and kneeling down they said the hymn, "Veni Creator"

(Come, O Holy Ghost), the antiphon, "Salve Regina" (Hail, holy Queen), and several other prayers. Then Blessed Giles blessed the boy, and saying good-bye, they went on their way.

About three years afterwards Blessed Giles, having gone to the monastery at Poitiers, a young novice just professed came to him, and weeping for joy, kneeling down, said, "Do you not know me again, Father?" Blessed Giles looked upon the youthful, upturned face, and answered: "Dear brother, I recollect having seen your face, but where, I do not remember." Then the youth said, "Do you not remember the little Peter, who served you in the Castle of Saint Maxentius, and for whom you prayed on your bended knees?" Overjoyed to meet his young benefactor once more, in the Dominican habit too, he tenderly embraced him, and gave him useful and loving advice on the way of keeping the rule, and the best means to acquire the perfection of a true religious spirit.

The talents of the servant of God were of great use to his native country. The king, Don Sancho II., having unhappily given himself up to the will of his favorites, was deprived of the administration of his kingdom, but not deposed. His brother, Don Alphonsus, was appointed regent of the kingdom, but many flew to arms in favor of King Sancho, and a civil war ensued. Blessed Giles, although he took no part in these sad divisions, was yet employed by the Papal Legate to preach the duty of submission, which shows us at the same time, the estimation he was held in, and his influence among the people.

Among the favorites of Don Sancho was one Martin Rool, who seeing the effect of the preaching of the saint upon the people, tried to close his mouth, and when he found he could not do that, covered him with abuse. The saint silently and patiently listened, and then turning to his fellow Dominican, Father Andrew, said: "Believe me, dear brother, a very horrible and violent end shortly awaits this man, which he will not be able to escape." This prediction was accomplished a short time after, for Martin Rool was hung by command of the King.

This task of preaching adherence to the

Regent Alphonsus, which was laid upon him by the Papal Legate, was certainly a difficult one; and a most conclusive proof of his success is given us in the fact that he continued the friend both of the semi-deposed King and of the Regent at the same time. Blessed Giles showed great respect for the unfortunate King, Don Sancho, although he knew it was his duty to uphold Don Alphonsus, and when all the King's former courtiers and favorites deserted him in his misfortunes, he continued to visit him in his retirement at Galicia and Toledo, to console him in his troubles. After his death, Don Alphonsus was crowned king. He gave Blessed Giles every mark of favor; he loved to talk with him, especially when he found himself in any trouble or difficulty. He built a beautiful church and convent for the Dominican Fathers at Lisbon, where he was afterwards buried.

We cannot but regret that the authors of the life of Blessed Giles, have not spoken at greater length of the public services he rendered to his country. They content themselves with saying, in a few words, that he labored much for the salvation of souls, for the increase and spiritual pefection of his Order, that he founded many monasteries, and sent Dominican missionaries to preach the faith in Tunis and other parts of Northern Africa. Whereas we know, that as he lived in days when ecclesiastics played a prominent part in politics, and as he was the friend and confidential adviser of two kings, we may feel sure that his influence made itself felt in the public administration of the kingdom.

After having been Provincial of Spain and Portugal eight years, from 1234 to 1242, he resigned his office so that he might attend exclusively to the care of his own soul, and labor for the salvation of sinners. He often said that it is very foolish to labor for the salvation of the souls of others and neglect one's own. But at the same time he knew that he would fall far short of his duty as a child of the apostolic St. Dominic, if he did not work incessantly for the good of souls. So after his resignation he continued for years to sanctify his own soul by prayer and penance, and to impart the fruit of his meditations to others, by constantly preaching and instructing the faithful.

He was succeeded in the provincialate by Father Peter d'Orca, after whose death he was again elected by the Fathers, who had not forgotten his labors in his first term of office. Although he was now aged and full of infirmities, he gave way again before the wishes of his brothers, and accepted the office a second time. He once more showed the same zeal for the good of the province, which had distinguished his first provincialate. He paid particular attention to the education of the novices, and to their studies, especially that of Holy Scriptures, and, as far as lay in his power, encouraged the apostolic spirit among the Fathers of the province, and his care was rewarded by a number of learned, holy and devoted religious in every monastery of Spain and Portugal.

He again visited all the monasteries of Spain and Portugal, and having come to Barcelona, spent several days in friendly conversation with Saint Raymond of Pennafort. From that town he set sail for the island of Majorca, to make a visitation of the Dominican monasteries there. But as the ship was just putting out of port, one of the passengers sneezed. This was looked upon, by the sailors, as an evil omen, and several of the passengers asked the captain of the vessel to return to land, to wait several days before commencing the voyage again. But Blessed Giles laughed at the miserable superstition, and told them it was quite contrary to the spirit of christianity to give faith to such absurdities. So from shame, rather than from inclination, the captain ordered the sailors to continue the voyage.

But hardly had the coast faded from their sight, than a fearful storm arose, and in a little time hope died in the hearts of all, except that of the saint. The ship was filled with confusion, and the passengers gave themselves up for lost. But the saint knew well that God would never allow them to be lost, and prayed with all the fervor of his soul, taking little heed of the angry murmurs of the superstitious sailors, who laid their misfortune at his door for having persuaded the captain to continue the voyage.

One of the passengers, a merchant of Barcelona, more furious against him than the rest, proposed to throw him into the sea like another Jonas.

Then Blessed Giles, raising his eyes towards the darkened heavens, prayed thus: "Can it be pleasing to Thee, O Lord, that we should be drowned in this raging storm of the sea, and that this evil soothsayer should conquer? O Lord Jesus, whose arm is as powerful to save on sea as on land, I beseech Thee to help Thy servants." Scarcely had he ended this prayer when the storm suddenly ceased. The sailors and passengers, astonished at this wonderful miracle, threw themselves at his feet and begged his pardon. But he who had been the foremost to accuse him of the expected shipwreck, with tears in his eyes, begged him to forget and forgive the wrong he had done him, and asked him to pray to God to forgive him his sin. "I will pardon you," said Blessed Giles, "if you will pardon him who has offended you."

Now it happened that this merchant had been wounded on the head by one of his fellow citizens, his near relation, and for a long time the two had been deadly enemies, to the scandal of the whole city. The Bishop had offered his friendly services to put an end to their quarrel, but without result, and the wounded man was only awaiting a favorable opportunity to take vengeance upon his enemy. Miraculous delivery from the danger of death did what nothing else could have done, and, at the wish of Blessed Giles, he forgave his enemy.

CHAPTER IV.

IN the island of Majorca, Blessed Giles found a large field for apostolic labors. Many sad superstitions, which had been left there by the Mahometans, were rife among its inhabitants, Majorca had but recently come under the dominion of the kings of Arragon, and a little band of Dominicans had been sent there a short time before Blessed Giles' visit, with the especial mission of restoring a purer spirit of christianity When the servant of God arrived, he at once set about preaching, and aided by his fellow religious, completely changed the people, so that when he left the island, he had rooted out all which was contrary to the pure morality of the christian faith.

After his return to Spain he was called to attend the general Chapter of the Dominican Order, held at Treves, in the year 1249. He took the opportunity of resigning his provincialate a second time. He had never forgotten the godless life he had led as a youth, before his conversion, and looked upon himself as unfit to rule others; and it is even said that he thought himself quite unfit to be one of the holy and innocent men who gathered together in chapter from all parts of Europe, although it may be doubted if there were any there dearer to God than he. His age and his many infirmities, made it necessary for him to have dispensations, and he could no longer make his journies on foot, like the other provincials. This he said must cause scandal to his brothers, and he thought it was his duty to resign his office. The Fathers accepted it out of deference to his wishes, much to his delight, for he could now spend the remainder of his life—fast drawing to an end—in quiet, and in labors for the salvation of souls, free from the duties of an important office.

When the Chapter was over he returned to Portugal, and retired to the monastery of Santarem, where he was daily beseiged by men of all states and conditions of life, who came to consult him about the state of their souls.

Sinners for counsel and direction, nobles, officers of the court, ecclesiastics, and common people, all came to him to ask his advice, or to commend themselves to his prayers. The King, Don Alphonsus, who loved the saint much, built a hermitage in a garden surrounded with high walls, near the saint's cell, so that he could retire there frequently, and from time to time enjoy the pleasure of his society.

Heretofore we have said but little about the many and wonderful ecstacies, visions, and spiritual graces of this great servant of God. Happily his biographers have left us ample details of his remarkable graces. They tell us that his love for God was so intense, that he was seized with a desire so vehement for heaven, that he was often obliged to keep his bed. He was frequently raised from the ground in ecstacy when in prayer; whatever position he was in, whether kneeling, whether bent downwards, erect, or standing, or with hands outstretched, it was all the same, the ardor of his soul was too strong for his body, and he was insensibly carried upwards. And when anyone happened to find him in this state he sighed and sobbed like a child taken from its nurse, when they brought him to himself.

Father Peter d'Orca, who succeeded him as Provincial after his first resignation, having come to the monastery of Santarem, the Fathers told him about the saintly life and remarkable ecstacies with which God favored the saint. But he was loath to believe all he heard. Now it so happened that one day Blessed Giles remained in the choir praying after the other Fathers had retired to their various occupations, and a short time afterwards was found in a state of ecstacy by some of the Fathers, who at once ran to tell the Provincial, so that he could see with his own eyes the favors God bestowed upon his chosen servant.

When he came to the place and saw the Blessed, he was much astonished, but wishing to test the reality of his ecstacy, put his ears to the saint's mouth and nostrils, to see if he breathed; not a sound could he hear; he was just as if dead. Then he took a hammer, and struck several stout raps upon a little table near, but there was not a movement or sign of consciousness. Then he took hold of him and pulled him violently from side to side, but with the same result. Then the Provincial burst into tears, and said, "Let us leave him to himself, happy in his ecstacy. His blessed soul has chosen the better part, which I think it is unjust to take from him ;" and he went away, leaving the saint still wrapped in contemplation.

Upon another occasion Father Peter Joannides, going to the saint's cell, found him raised in the air, with his arms stretched out to heaven, above a table on which lay an open book which proved to be the works of St. Denis. The Father tried to pull him down, but in vain; so leaving him in his trance, he went to call the Prior, and not being able to find him at hand, came across Father Peter Crutius and Father Alphonsus of Tolosa, and with them returned to the saint's cell. But when they opened the door they found him quietly seated at his table reading.

Father Peter was much disappointed at not having seen the ecstasy, and attributed it, in his humility, to his unworthiness. But in due time he was amply rewarded by the sight of an ecstasy no less wonderful. He remained in the choir one evening after Complin, and when he had finished his prayer went to Blessed Giles' cell, and opening the door saw the saint suspended in the open air, outside his cell window, his hands folded over his face. The Father ran at once and brought the sub-prior, Father Mark, who, taking hold of the saint, with much difficulty, aided by Father Peter, drew him into the cell, and having placed him upon his bed, "left him," so says the old writer, "to repose with his beloved Jesus."

Many other wonderful ecstasies are narrated in his life, but there is one which we cannot omit here. About twenty years before his death, being in the monastery at Santarem, he remained as usual in the choir to pray after the Office, and feeling that he would soon be drawn out of himself in ecstasy, and not wishing to be seen, went into the sacristy and sat down there. Now, there was a door opening from the church into the sacristy, and in this door a little lattice,

Blessed Giles of Santarem.

which was used to pass out anything the people asked for from the sacristy, and it so happened that, just at the moment when Blessed Giles seated in the sacristy, was carried away in spirit to the presence of God, a pious woman, Elvira Duranda, came to this little lattice door, most likely to ask for something, and, peeping through, saw the saint in ecstasy. She looked at him in astonished silence, and, after some time, saw, as it were, a column of heavenly light descend upon him, which so illuminated his body that it seemed like a crystal when the sun shines upon it. She gazed at this wonderful sight a long time, until at last the light died away, and Blessed Giles, breathing a mournful sigh, came round and, as if dazzled by the brightness with which he had been clothed, began to grope about with his hands outstretched to find the way out of the sacristy. She kept this incident a secret until the death of the saint, when she revealed it to Father Bernard Morleus, a Dominican Father, whose beautiful history, and that of his two little disciples, is well known.

Blessed Giles was once laid on his bed in the monastery at Lisbon, when the very heavens were opened to his sight, and he saw Jesus and Mary with his bodily eyes. At which, although he was usually very grave and sedate in manner, he laughed out aloud in his glee, and cried out: "O my Jesus! O sweetest Jesus! O Jesus, whose name deservest to be written and carried in the heart! O Mary, most meek, most loving Mother of our Lord; O most glorious Virgin, Queen of heaven and earth, how can I, a miserable sinner, give you thanks?"

He repeated these words several times with his eyes turned towards heaven, when Father Peter, who slept above, hearing him, ran down to see what caused him to cry out aloud. "What is it, Father Giles?" he said, "why do you laugh? why do you clap your hands? what do you see? But Blessed Giles said to him: "Go away, Brother and sleep, what business is it of yours?" and so the poor Father was obliged to return to his bed, knowing only from what he had heard, that the saint had seen our Blessed Lord and his immaculate Mother.

During his life, and after his death, Blessed Giles was the instrument in the hand of God to work many miracles, but was more especially gifted in obtaining by his prayers the blessing of children for barren women.

He had a very remarkable and tender devotion to the most holy name of Jesus; that name "whose sweetness," to use St. Bernard's words, "fills the heart." As often as he heard it spoken by others, or spoke it himself, as he often did, a sweetness beyond description flooded his soul. One day he went to the monastery infirmary to see Father Martin of Lisbon, who was ill, and as they were talking, the sick Father let fall the name of Jesus; it at once shook the saint to the center of his soul, and he said: "Do you know, Brother, how sweet a name you have spoken? Jesus! Jesus!" and repeating it he arose and partly leaning on a staff he carried, and not ceasing to pronounce the holy name, in the sight of all present, fell into a profound ecstacy, in which he neither felt or heard anything for a long time.

Now there was in the convent at that time a

certain Father Vincent, of Lisbon, who had been the King's physician. He had never yet seen the saint in ecstacy, and could not be brought to believe what the Fathers told him, so some of them went to call him to come and see with his own eyes the wonders God showered upon Blessed Giles. When he came to the infirmary, and saw him leaning upon his staff, wrapt in silent contemplation, he went up to him and suddenly pulled the staff away, in such a manner that Blessed Giles ought to have fallen, but finding that he remained in exactly the same position, not moving in the least, he tried several other tests, even that of putting a lighted candle to the tips of the saint's fingers, but with the same result, and at last he was forced to admit that there was no deception, and that his was in truth a real ecstacy.

Blessed Giles lived to a ripe old age. At last he was attacked by a slight illness, and knowing by divine revelation the hour of his approaching death, caused a hair shirt to be put upon his weakened and emaciated body, and having very devoutly received the last sacraments of the church, and spoken sweet words of comfort to his sorrowing brethren, he stretched out his hands to heaven, and in a loud voice cried out: "Into Thy hands O Lord, I commend my spirit." Then, with his body in the form of a cross, without any agony, this holy penitent entered into his rest. It was the feast of the Ascension, May 15th, 1265.

His venerable body, which had been cleansed from the sins of his erring youth in the fiery baptism of penance, was preserved incorrupt, and sent forth a sweet perfume. The Fathers took the heavy iron chain he had worn, from his body, and kept it as a precious relic; it has been the means of giving fecundity to numberless childless women.

Many miracles having been worked at his tomb, a cultus sprung up, and having continued without interruption, Pope Benedict XIV., approved of it, and granted a feast in honor of Blessed Giles, with a Mass and Office, to the Dominican Order, and to the dioceses of Lisbon and Viseau. The inhabitants of Santarem number him among their principal patrons. His feast is kept on the 14th of May in the Dominican Order, and on the Sunday after the Ascension in the diocese of Viseau.

BLESSED BERTRAND OF GARRIGUE.

BLESSED BERTRAND OF GARRIGUE.

THE LATEST SAINT ADDED TO THE DOMINICAN CALENDAR.

BLESSED Bertrand was born in the 12th century in the little town of Garrigue, in the diocese of Nimes, in the South of France.

We are, unhappily, left in complete ignorance of the names and condition of his parents, and of the events of his early life. The first incident we know is that he gave himself to the service of God, was ordained priest, and acted as a missionary in Languedoc. That part of France was in a very disturbed state, owing to the ravages of the Albigensian heretics, and stood sorely in need of generous and devoted souls, such as his, to show the people by example, as well as by word, the truth and beauty of the ancient Catholic faith, which the heretics had done much to root out and destroy.

Since the mere mention of heresy often excites, even in the hearts of Catholics, a certain sympathy, owing chiefly to the exaggerated accounts, given by Protestant historians, of persecution endured by heretics at the hands of Catholics, and also partly to a decay of solid appreciation of Catholic truth, it will be well to give some account of the Albigensian heresy, and what it taught.

It received its name from a district in southern France, surrounding the town of Albi, whose inhabitants were called Albigeois. They taught as a fundamental doctrine, that all things were created by the evil spirit; they abstained from all animal food except fish, looking upon it and matter as evil in their nature. Some of them entirely abjured marriage as sinful, while others allowed it provided the bride was a virgin, and the husband and wife separated after the birth of the first child; and, on the contrary, many of them indulged in the most revolting immorality, as a natural consequence of their principles.

They also taught that the souls of men are fallen spirits, who were all created at one time, but are now condemned to pass from one body to another, until by the practice of good works they are purified, and are restored to their original state. They maintained that the guilt of every sin is equal, and that all are deserving of death, but that punishment for sin is inflicted in this life only.

Others denied the immortality of the soul, and the existence of spiritual things. Many taught absolute fatalism, and denied free will, both in man and God, in so far as it extends to the knowledge of good and evil, and the power of preventing evil.

As well as these errors, this heresy had also a political side, and was imbued with the spirit of revolution and sedition. Its followers ravaged the country, set fire to the churches, tortured priests and nuns, trampled the most adorable sacrament of the altar under foot, and committed every other conceivable violence.

To recall these misled people to the bosom of the Church, Pope Innocent III., sent a commission entirely composed of Cistercians—Arnold, Abbot of Citeaux, and two papal legates, Rodolph and Peter of Castelnau, accompanied by several other Abbots. This commission totally failed, partly on account of the overwhelming influence which Count Raymond of Tolouse exercised against them, and also much more on account of the evil example of many of the Catholic bishops and priests, who led a very worldly and unedifying life. The heretics pointed to the lives of these unworthy clergy, and, affecting great austerity of life themselves, contrasted their own practice with that of the Catholic priests, much of course to their own advantage. Alas! that the shepherds of Christ's flock should cause the sheep to go astray—yet so it was. "The heretics," says Blessed Jordan of Saxony, "attracted men by persuasion, by preaching, and outward show of holiness, whilst the legates were surrounded by a large suite of followers, horses, and rich apparel. They failed therefore, as was only to be expected; the poor and simple never have been and never will be converted by pomp and display of worldly influence. To them an evangelical life is the best proof of a mission from on high, the lowly beauty of holiness, the meekness of a truly mortified and crucified man, touches their hearts; but claims to superiority will usually meet with indifference and contempt.

At length the missionaries and the leaders of the Catholic party recognized their want of success, and met at Montpellier, to try and discover some means by which they could touch the hearts of the deluded people. Whilst they were deliberating, they heard of the arrival of Diego of Azevedo, Prior of the Augustinian canons of the cathedral of Osma, and his Sub-Prior, Father Dominic Guzman. They were on their return from a pilgrimage to Rome, and, having visited the Abbey of Citeaux, were accompanied by several Cistercians. The reputation for sanctity which Don Diego and Father Dominic had already acquired, caused the Catholic missionaries to send to ask their assistance at the conference. When the matter was laid before them, Diego solved the difficulty at once; "do, as I am going to do," he said, and immediately he dismissed his attendants and followers. "Live a poor and austere life," was the advice he gave them, "and then we shall be able to convert the people, so easily moved by example, and so very deaf to arguments and outward show." They took his advice, and thus a little company of ecclesiastics was formed, among whom was St. Dominic. They at once set out for Tolouse, preaching the Catholic faith as they went along, and reconciling large numbers of those who had wandered away from the true faith.

Thus was begun the marvellous mission of St. Dominic against the Albigensian heresy; for he soon came to be looked upon as the head and leading spirit of the movement, Diego of Azevedo having in the meantime returned to Spain, and the Cistercians to their Abbeys. For ten years, St. Dominic and his companions, who were joined by Blessed Bertrand, labored with zeal and success to restore the faith in the province of Narbonne.

During the lamentable war which was at length provoked by the excesses of the heretics,

St Dominic and his companions continued the same apostolic life of preaching from village to village and town to town, and they began to be known as the "Preaching Brothers," although as yet they were not a regularly constituted religious Order. At the end of the war, six in number, they went together to Tolouse, where St. Dominic began the foundation of the Dominican Order. In that city they were received into the house of a rich citizen, Peter Cellani, who joined them and lived there under a regular rule of life. In the year 1215, St. Dominic went to Rome with the Bishop of Tolouse, to attend the Council of Lateran. He seized the opportunity of laying the idea of his new Order before Pope Innocent III., but as the Council had just made a decree, ordaining that those who in future wished to become religious, must join an Order already approved by the Church, and not found a new one, Innocent bade him take council with his Brothers, and adopt some rule, already flourishing in the Church.

When St. Dominic returned to Prouille, he

found the number of his community increased to sixteen: Matthew of France, William de Claret, Brother Noel, Suero Gomes, Michael de Fabra, Michael de Uzero, Brother Dominic, called " Little Brother Dominic," Laurence the Englishman, Stephen of Metz, John of Navarre, Peter of Madrid, Thomas of Tolouse, Oderic of Normandy, a lay Brother, Manez Guzman, brother of St. Dominic, and Bertrand of Garrigues. They chose the rule of St. Augustine.

When St. Dominic returned to Rome, to report their decision, he left Blessed Bertrand Superior of the house in his absence, a sign of the eminent holiness of our saint, and of the high opinion St. Dominic had of his abilities.

Pope Innocent III. having died, his successor, Honorius III. solemnly approved the newly founded Order of Friar Preachers.

On St. Dominic's return to Tolouse, 1217, he received the vows of the sixteen Brothers in the chapel of the Dominican nun's convent, at Prouille. This done, he immediately sent them into different countries, to spread the Order, and to preach to the people. Blessed Bertrand, with

Blessed Bertrand of Garrigue. 167

six others, was sent to found a monastery in Paris. At first their success was very small, and ten months were spent in the direst poverty and want, but in the August of 1218, John de Barastre, a professor in the university of Paris, and chaplain to the King, obtained for them a little church, dedicated to St. James, to which a hospital for strangers was attached. This in time became one of the most famous monasteries of the whole Order.

Soon after this, Blessed Bertrand must have returned to Tolouse, for we find that when St. Dominic returned from another visit to Italy, coming to Tolouse he nominated Blessed Bertrand Prior of the community. The saint also chose him for his traveling companion on a journey to Paris made soon after. This monastery of St. Romain at Tolouse was the first founded in the Order, and thus Blessed Bertrand was the first Dominican Prior, after St. Dominic. Peter Cellani's house having become too small for them, a poor but monastic cloister had been built near the church of St. Romain, which had been given to them by Fulk, Bishop of Tolouse, and very humble, small cells built over it for the brethren. Blessed Bertrand remained Prior of this lowly community until the year 1221, when he was elevated to a still higher office in the Order. In that year the second Chapter of Bologna was held. Sixty monasteries had already been founded, and very many more were in process of erection. St. Dominic in this Chapter divided the Order into eight provinces: Spain, Tolouse, France, Lombardy, Rome, Germany, Hungary and England, and appointed a Prior Provincial for each. Blessed Bertrand was chosen by him as Provincial of Tolouse, which comprised the whole of the South of France, from the Pyrenees to the Alps, and was the largest of all the newly constituted provinces. Thus St. Dominic again showed in a very marked way his especial esteem for the virtues and abilities of Blessed Bertrand.

He fulfilled the duties of his new office with energy, and largely increased the number of monasteries in the province. He had always been a man of prayer and great mortification, and never allowed the duties of the offices he held to mitigate them. The lofty idea which Blessed Bertrand had of the supreme sanctity of God, made him look upon the slightest fault as worthy of great punishment, and he wept for his sins so frequently, that St. Dominic, fearing excess, and wishing to test his obedience, bade him moderate those outward signs of sorrow for sin, and not to weep, except for the conversion of sinners. He obeyed, for he was well grounded in humility He began to say many prayers for the conversion of sinners, and to say Mass every day for the same intention.

Surius relates the following beautiful anecdote of our Saint. "Being asked by one, Brother Benedict, a man of prudence, why he so rarely said Mass for the dead, and so frequently for sinners, he replied: 'We are certain of the salvation of the faithful departed, whereas *we* remain tossed about in many perils.' 'Then if there were two beggars,' said Brother Benedict, 'the one with all his limbs sound, the other wanting them, which would you compassionate the most?' Father Bertrand answered: 'I should certainly compassionate most him who could do least for himself.' 'Then,' answered Brother Benedict, 'the dead are such, for they have neither mouth to confess, nor hands to work, but ask our help, whereas on the contrary, living sinners have mouths and hands, and with them can take care of themselves.' And when Blessed Bertrand was not persuaded in his mind, the next night a terrible figure of a departed soul appeared to him, who with a bundle of wood in a wonderful manner pressed and weighed upon him, and waking him more than ten times, vexed and troubled him. On the following morning, he called Brother Benedict, and told him, and then with many tears, going to the altar he offered the holy sacrifice for the departed and often did the same from that time."

Being so constantly the companion of St. Dominic on his apostolic journeyings, he was several times the witness of and co-worker in that saint's miracles. Thus, one day, as they were walking along near Carcassonne, it beginning to rain, St. Dominic made the sign of the cross over the elements, and although torrents fell all around them, neither was even so much as touched by the drops, and passed through the storm perfectly dry. This miracle was told by Blessed Bertrand to Blessed Jordan of Saxony, who relates it.

Brother Gerard de Frachet in his "Lives of the Brothers," tells us in the following words another striking miracle. "The Blessed Father, going from Tolouse to Paris, passing through Roc-Amadour, spent the night devoutly in the church of Blessed Mary, having a companion devout and holy, Brother Bertrand, who was the first Prior Provincial of the Brothers of the Province.

"But, the next day, they had as companions on the way, some German pilgrims, who hearing them saying psalms and litanies, piously followed them, and coming to a village invited them, and according to their usual manner, graciously provided for their wants, and this they did for four consecutive days. On the fourth day, Blessed Dominic, in tears, said to his companion, Brother Bertrand, 'Truly, I am troubled in conscience, that we should reap the carnal things of these pilgrims, when we do not spiritually sow for them, therefore, if it please you, let us pray to the Lord on bended knees, that He may both give us understanding and use of their language, so that we may be able to announce the Lord Jesus to them.'

"Which, when they had done, they spoke German, to the great amazement of the pilgrims, and traveling four other days with them talking with them of the Lord Jesus, came to Orleans. But when the said Germans wished to go to Chartres, they left them on the road to Paris, commending themselves to their prayers.

"But one day the Blessed Father said to Brother Bertrand, "Behold Brother, when we enter Paris if the Brothers should get to know the miracle which the Lord worked for us, they will think we are saints, whereas we are sinners; and if it should come to the knowledge of seculars, we shall suffer much from vanity, wherefore I forbid you, under obedience, to say anything about it before my death.

"After the death of the Blessed Father, the aforesaid Brother Bertrand, devoutly narrated this to the Brothers."

Such are the chief events in the life of this servant of God; we can only lament that we know no more, and that so little has come down to us of the secrets of his inner life, the life of the soul, that which draws the broad line of distinction between the saint, and those who lead holy lives indeed, but do not rise higher than the practice of the virtues necessary to the ordinary christian.

It only remains now to mention his death, burial, and the events connected with his memory and cultus.

His duties as Provincial of Provence did not hinder his devoting himself to apostolic work, preaching missions, and converting sinners. On one of these apostolic quests, he came to Bouschet, a town in the diocese of Valence, for the purpose of preaching to a flourishing community of Cistercian Sisters. While there he was taken sick and died, in the year 1230. His body was buried in the cemetery attached to the convent, with great ceremony. Bernard Guidonis, quoted by Malvenda, says that it was exhumed twenty-three years afterwards, when it was found entire and incorrupt. It was afterwards solemnly translated to Orange, and was finally burnt by the heretics in the sixteenth century.

Malvenda says that in his own time, several miracles were wrought at the saint's tomb, and that the inhabitants of Bouschet preserved a great devotion towards him, and always spoke of him as *Saint* Bertrand. An ancient statue, which is supposed to be of him, is religiously preserved in the church to this day.

His cultus having continued without interruption, Pope Leo XIII. ratified it, and granted permission to the Dominican Order and to the clergy of the dioceses of Valence and Nimes, to keep his feast with Mass and Office.

The Venerable Bartholomew of the Martyrs.

THE VENERABLE BARTHOLOMEW OF THE MARTYRS.

CHAPTER I.

THE name of Bartholomew of the Martyrs is familiar to those who are acquainted with Church History, as that of one of the glories of the sixteenth century, and one of the best known and most influential of the Fathers of the Council of Trent. It is as a great Bishop and Reformer of abuses that he is best known, and his life is a beautiful example of the active side of the religious character. But, as no true love for souls can exist apart from the love of God, we find that he was as good a religious as he was a great and prudent prelate, and that his zeal for others was founded upon a life of purity and union with God.

He was the friend of St. Charles Borromeo, who gave him peculiar marks of his veneration and confidence. In the Council of Trent his influence was very great; and he was undoubtedly one of the foremost of that host of great and holy men, whom God in His mercy raised up to defend his Church, at the time when the rise of Protestantism seemed to threaten its very life.

Bartholomew de Valle was born at Lisbon, the Capital of Portugal, in the year 1514. His parents were of good family, and very pious Catholics. Their favorite virtue was charity to the poor, and though their means were but small, they contrived by great economy to give abundant alms.

Bartholomew was baptized in the Church of the Martyrs, and as he esteemed his regeneration by baptism far beyond his natural birth, he preferred to be known by the name of the Church where he had received this grace rather than by his family name. Hence it is that he was always called Bartholomew of the Martyrs.

From his earliest years he always showed himself grave, modest, gentle, and obedient. His parents taught him to join in their exercises of piety and charity, and his mother often made him the bearer of her gifts to persons who, from a higher position, had fallen into poverty, for she especially loved to bestow her alms on such as these.

Thus, as Bartholomew grew in age, so he advanced in virtue, and the Holy Ghost hastened to draw him, by a special vocation, to His service, before the world could corrupt him. He was less than fifteen years old when he was attracted to the Order of St. Dominic by the apostolic preaching of its religious. His parents were too pious to offer any opposition to his desires, and he therefore received the habit of the Order in the convent of St. Dominic, at Lisbon, on the feast of St. Martin, 1528.

He passed his year of noviciate with great fervor. The world he had left seemed to him a prison from which he had escaped, and the religious life a paradise which had been opened to him, and he felt full of wonder and gratitude that so great a grace should have been bestowed on him. He was remarkable for his humility, and he was never better satisfied than when low and humble duties were imposed upon him. It seemed to him that those words of our Lord (Luke xiv. 10), "When thou art invited, go, sit down in the lowest place," were addressed especially to him, and he ever looked on himself as being the last and lowest in the house.

But his principal devotion was to adore and imitate the sufferings of our Lord, and to withdraw himself into His wounds as into a place of safety; it was from this devotion that he obtained that fortitude and spirit of mortification which characterized him for the rest of his life. When he fell into any little fault he received with such sweetness the correction which was given him, that he never lost his peace of mind, and his falls, instead of doing him harm, served to render him more humble, and more watchful over himself.

After his profession, which he made on November 20th, 1529, he was occupied for several years in studying philosophy and theology In these studies he showed great quickness of apprehension, and no less diligence and application. He was careful to accompany his studies with much prayer, as well as with meditation on the Holy Scriptures, in which he took great delight. He had a much greater love for theology than for philosophy, because in it his mind was occupied about God and His attributes and mysteries.

Bartholomew finished his studies, by defending public theses in a Provincial Chapter of his Order held in Guimaraes. He was then appointed to teach others the sciences of which he had hitherto been a student, and he continued to be so employed, partly at Lisbon, and partly in the celebrated monastery of Batalha, for nearly twenty years. He was also occupied in preaching, and in the fulfillment of this office he showed that he possessed a truly apostolic spirit. He kept continually in his mind our Lord's words about St. John Baptist, "He was a burning and a shining light" (John 5, v. 35), wishing thus to remind himself, that in order to give light to others, a man must first himself burn with the love of God and of souls.

His life passed very peacefully in the fulfillment of these duties, and in the observances of the religious life. In the latter he was most fervent; he availed himself of no exemption nor dispensation, and never allowed his occupations, however numerous and pressing they might be, to keep him from the exercises of the religious life, or to disturb his recollection of soul.

Very few notable events broke the even course of his life. In 1558 he defended public theses of theology in the General Chapter of Salamanca, and was made Master in Theology by the General of the Order, and the following year he was elected Definitor It was about the same time that he was appointed professor of theology to one of the sons of Dom Louis, brother of the King of Portugal, who desired to embrace the ecclesiastical state. This office was a great trial to him, for it obliged him to go to Evora, where the King and his court then were, and this interfered with his retirement, and brought him into contact with the world. It was at this time that he composed a collection of Maxims of the Saints, no doubt in order to fortify his soul against the new temptations and difficulties to which he was exposed.

He had been two years at Evora when he was elected Prior of the Convent of his order at Bemfica, a suburb of Lisbon. The Prince Dom Louis did not oppose his accepting the office, but he wished that his son should go to reside near the convent, in order that he might continue to profit by the lessons of F. Bartholomew.

All the energy of the new Prior was directed to the spiritual good of his community. His principal care was to encourage his religious to detachment from self and to lead them to the love of God by continual prayer. He did not devote special attention to their exterior demeanor, for, as he was accustomed to say, if the soul were full of God, the outward bearing would be sure to correspond to what was within. His chief love and care were lavished upon the novices, and the spiritual lectures and exercises he frequently gave them were so touching that they often moved them to tears.

His office of tutor to the son of the Prince Dom Louis had made him intimate with the royal family, and he frequently received visits from some of its members in the convent. They were greatly edified by the strictness of the house, and often made presents of considerable value to the Prior. The convent, however, was none the richer for these offerings, for F. Bartholomew had no idea of laying up treasures on earth, and for the most part such gifts were distributed to the poor. He did not even content himself with this, but added to his alms out of the property of the convent, and once, in time of scarcity, caused the dinner that had been prepared for the community to be distributed to the poor who had come to ask alms at the convent gate. Evidently the lessons of charity that had been taught him by his mother had not been forgotten.

But while F. Bartholomew was thus living in the retirement of his monastery, desirous only of avoiding the world, and of serving God unknown to men, God was preparing to bring him forth from his obscurity, and to make use of him for the advantage of a vast number of souls, and for the general good of the Church.

CHAPTER II.

AT the beginning of the year 1558, the Archbishopric of Braga, the Primatial see of Portugal, became vacant by the death of Archbishop Limpo. The celebrated Father Lewis of Granada was at this time Provincial of the Dominicans in Portugal, and at the height of his reputation for learning and holiness. He was at once proposed for the vacant dignity, but declined it, and no entreaties could shake his constant refusal. The Queen Regent, finding that she could not induce him to yield, placed the choice of the future Archbishop in his hands. F. Lewis well knew the sterling worth of Bartholomew, and recommended him to the Queen as the most fitting person to fill the high office.

Meanwhile, Bartholomew had heard that the archbishopric had been offered to F. Lewis, and had written to him to persuade him not to accept it, on account of the danger so high and responsible an office brings with it. We can, therefore, imagine his sore dismay when he heard that he himself had been appointed, at F. Lewis' recommendation, to fill the sacred but dangerous post. He declined it resolutely, and his resistance was only overcome by a formal command from the Provincial, obliging him to accept under pain of excommunication.

Bartholomew therefore submitted to his fate, but his obedience cost him dear, for his anxiety caused a severe illness which brought him near to death.

As soon as his health permitted he set out for the Court of Lisbon. When he had arrived at the gates of the palace, he sat down upon a stone to rest. While he was thus seated, the Duke of Avero drove up to demand an audience of the Queen Regent. He had come to ask that F. Bartholomew's appointment be cancelled, and the vacant dignity given to his own nephew. While he was on a balcony waiting to see the Queen, a gentleman asked him whether he would like to see the new Archbishop of Braga, and pointed to F. Bartholomew, who was sitting at the gate below. The Duke was touched by the humble and grave demeanour of F. Bartholomew, and instead of making the request he had intended, thanked the Queen for having appointed so worthy a subject to the archbishopric.

Bartholomew's illness had caused his consecration to be deferred. He received his Bulls from Pope Paul IV. in 1559, and on the 3d of September of that year, was consecrated in the Church of St. Dominic at Lisbon, where he had received the religious habit thirty-one years before.

A few days later he set out for his diocese, in great poverty and simplicity, rather like the apostles of old, than a rich prelate of the 16th century. He was accompanied by two of his brethren in religion—F. John de Leira and F. Henry de Tavora. The latter had been one of his community at Bemfica, and afterwards became Archbishop of Goa, in India.

He arrived at Braga on the 4th of October, and was received with universal joy and satisfaction. He found the archiepiscopal palace very little to his taste; its grand rooms, with their paintings and ornaments, displeased his love of poverty and simplicity. He therefore closed them, and chose for his own use a small room with bare walls, furnished with a plain wooden table and a bed composed of three boards laid on trestles. This bed was very short and, as Bartholomew was tall, he had to draw himself up in order to find room to lie upon it.

From the time that he came to Braga he adopted the following rule of life: He rose every morning at three o'clock, and from that hour until eight, when he said Mass, occupied himself in prayer, saying office, and reading the Holy Scriptures and the Fathers of the Church. After Mass he gave audience to the public, always taking care to admit the poor first. He dined at midday, and spent the afternoon in again receiving those who came on business. He ordinarily retired to his room when the Angelus rang at sunset, and putting aside all business, passed the evening in prayer and meditation. By nature he was very exact and business like, but he had received this grace from

God, that when he retired to his room his mind was quite free from all anxiety as to business matters, and could give its undivided attention to the things of God. If he was interrupted during the evening to attend to any pressing matter, he was accustomed to settle it in very few words, saying "Sufficient for the day is the evil of it," and he would add, that after giving the day to one's neighbors, it was but reasonable that the night should be reserved for God.

He was accustomed to continue his pious exercises until about 11 o'clock at night, and then he retired to rest, four hours' sleep being the utmost that he ever allowed himself.

His food was very simple and austere. Only one dish was served at his table, and this he divided into two parts, one of which he ate, and the other, sent to the poor. For it was his practice to invite our Blessed Lord to his table, and he considered it a great honor to be able to offer Him in the person of His poor a part of the gifts he had received from Him.

The former archbishops of Braga had been accustomed to maintain a large number of officials and servants in their palace, whose conduct had not always been very edifying. Bartholomew dismissed these useless attendants, and his household was composed only of persons of good life, whose services were necessary or useful. His stables contained but one mule, which he used on his journeys, and which at other times was employed in all sorts of work.

The income of his see was very large; he confided it to the administration of persons of great fidelity and honesty, and chose for his treasurer one who was full of charity for the poor, and fond of alms-giving. He had now the means of practicing that charity which he had learnt from his mother's example and teaching, and he speedily began to show how thoroughly it had taken possession of his soul.

When he made the first visitation of his diocese he informed himself in each parish as to the number and wants of the poor, and especially of those who had formerly been in good circumstances. He made a list of them, and caused alms to be distributed to them according to their needs. The number of poor people thus assisted by him was very large.

In the city of Braga, where he resided, he caused a still more exact account of the poor, to be kept, and especially of the widows and destitute young women of good conduct. So great was his care on this point, that no case of distress, however secret it might be, remained unknown to him, and he took special pains to find out cases of poverty in persons of respectable position. All the poor who were known to him received a stated allowance of food from him every week, and those of the better classes received alms in money every month ; and with such exactitude and regularity were these gifts bestowed, that no one ever received less than the appointed amount, nor was there ever any delay in their distribution.

He also paid house rent for many persons; and he maintained a doctor, at his own expense, to visit and attend on the sick poor. Moreover, every Wednesday and Friday money was distributed to all the poor who presented themselves at his palace, and the number of these was generally more than a thousand. On such occasions a priest was appointed by him to give them an instruction, for he held that spiritual alms deeds are of even greater worth than those which relieve the wants of the body.

He showed special charity to poor convents of monks and nuns, considering that services rendered to these who imitate the life of our Lord by their holy and self sacrificing lives, are in a special way rendered to our Lord Himself.

Very soon after his arrival in Braga he founded a hospital in the city, building it and maintaining it entirely at his own expense. He also established several infirmaries on a smaller scale; these also he provided with everything necessary for the sick, and he often visited them himself.

These good works were not done by the holy Archbishop out of the superabundance of his revenue. In order to be able to meet the vast expenses he thus incurred he was obliged to be very sparing in his other expenditure. A very small part of his income was spent on himself; we have seen how poorly his table was furnished, and he continued to wear the habit of his order, made of the same common material he had used when he was a simple religious. Several times he denied himself a new habit when he had need of it, in order that the materials might be used to make clothes for some poor person. Indeed, he looked upon his income as being held in trust for the benefit of the poor, and everything that was used for his own wants seemed to him to be so much taken from the necessitous to whom it of right belonged.

But the spiritual needs of his flock caused the good Archbishop much greater anxiety than the temporal wants of the poor. There is no doubt that at that time the diocese of Braga was in great need of the energetic labors of a prelate of holy life and animated with a great zeal for souls. The great evil from which it was suffering was the ignorance of the people, for ignorance is the mother of all vices; and the ignorance of the people was in great part due to the want of learned and zealous priests.

Bartholomew applied himself with great energy to remedying this evil. His first step was to make a personal visitation of his diocese, in order that he might obtain an exact knowledge of the condition and needs of his flock. It was very beautiful and edifying to his people to see the holy and humble prelate, traveling from town to town, and from village to village across mountains and valleys, riding Christlike on a mule, accompanied by one or two religious, enduring all this fatigue from pure and burning love of his ignorant flock, who were all full of faith, but sadly wanting in knowledge, and in too many cases addicted to lamentable superstitions.

It was no less beautiful to see how every scene through which he passed filled his soul with holy thoughts. When they crossed a mountain he would cry out in the words of holy Scripture, "Come, and let us go up to the mount of the Lord;" the desert places reminded him of the ancient hermits, and the solitudes in which they served God; rough ways drew from him expressions of the most perfect patience; while flowery meadows, rolling rivers, and shady woods, seemed to him to be so many voices of grateful nature praising God for His beauty.

Cold and hunger seemed powerless over him. One day a religious who accompanied him complained of the bitter cold: "Dear brother," he said, "the best way to keep warm is to pray." And, in fact, the warmth of his devotion did extend itself to his body.

When he arrived at any town or village he said Mass, and preached simple and instructive sermons to the people. He then received all those who came to speak to him, and afterwards visited the people in their own houses. He inquired into all the abuses and evil customs that existed in the place, and did his best to put an end to them, and was very earnest in endeavoring to reconcile those who were at enmity with one another, and in healing discords in families. He thus acquired an exact knowledge of the state of his diocese, a knowledge which was of the greatest possible service to him in governing his flock. His spiritual subjects too felt henceforth that the eye of their pastor was upon them, abuses began to be checked, and many souls were converted to God.

CHAPTER III.

SO soon as Bartholomew had concluded the visitation of a portion of his vast diocese (it contained no less than 1,400 parishes) he returned to Braga, to carry out those plans of reform with which the state of his diocese had inspired him. We have already said that the source of all these evils was ignorance, and that the ignorance of the flock was due to the lack of knowledge and zeal in the clergy.

The first remedy to those evils which suggested itself to the Archbishop was his own example. He began, therefore, to preach frequently to his people. He spoke to them without any affectation of learning or eloquence, and at the same time without over familiarity, but with the dignity of a bishop addressing the flock committed to him by God, and with the affection of a father speaking to the children whom he loves. His sermons were full of instruction on the points about which his people were most ignorant, and were directed against the vices which most prevailed amongst them. He prayed much before preaching, and therefore the voice of God spoke in his words, and carried light and conviction to the souls of his hearers. Vast numbers came to hear him, and they listened with the greater docility to his teaching, because they knew how poor, humble, and mortified his own life was.

He knew, however, that his own efforts were all insufficient to the accomplishment of the great work of reforming his diocese, and that it could only be accomplished by training a learned and zealous body of priests. He therefore chose learned and pious professors of his own order for the instruction of the young clergy in theology. He also took care to select pious and intelligent boys to be educated as priests, and provided the necessary funds for their support.

For the education of his people in general he established a college of the Society of Jesus at Braga. This great society was then at its commencement; but it already possessed one college in Portugal, that of Coimbra, which had become famous for the learning and holiness of those trained in it, and especially for the missioners sent from it to preach the faith in the East, chief of whom was St. Francis Xavier. Bartholomew was full of veneration for the holiness and zeal of that saint and his companions, and desired nothing more ardently than to procure for his diocese the advantage of possessing a college directed by members of their order, and animated by the same spirit. The Chapter of his Cathedral and the authorities of the city opposed the establishment of the Jesuit college, but the Archbishop overcame all these difficulties, and having applied to F. Lainez, the successor of St. Ignatius in the government of the Society, he obtained the fathers necessary for its foundation.

After Bartholomew had been in possession of the archbishopric for about a year and a half he was summoned to attend the Council of Trent

This celebrated Council, which had been occasioned by the rise and spread of the Protestant heresies, and by the desire of the Popes to reform the evils existing amongst Catholics, had been begun nearly sixteen years before, but had been thrice interrupted by the disasters of the times. Pope Pius IV. ordered it to be recommenced at Easter, 1561, and issued a Bull, summoning the bishops of the Church to assist at it, and to concert by their wisdom and prudence, enlightened by the Holy Spirit of God, those measures which should seem to them most proper to renew the faith and piety of the Christian people.

Immediately after receiving the Pope's summons, Bartholomew made the necessary arrangements for the government of his diocese during his absence, and set out for Trent. He was suffering at the time from a disease of the leg, which caused him great suffering, but he was not accustomed to allow such obstacles to hinder him from the discharge of any duty of his office, and, therefore, not permit this difficulty to keep him from this long and difficult journey. He was accompanied by F. Henry de Tavora and a small number of the most necessary attendants.

The way in which he made this journey is an

excellent illustration of his dislike of all display and of the attentions ordinarily paid to one of his high rank. When he came to a town where there was a convent of his order (and this was nearly always the case), he left his attendants to go by themselves to an inn, whilst he went to the convent, accompanied only by F. Henry de Tavora. He had laid aside all signs of his rank, and presented himself merely as an ordinary religious, who came to seek hospitality on his journey. There were at this time many fathers of the order on their way to the General Council, and therefore, generally speaking, but few questions were asked of the Archbishop and his companion, and his real dignity remained unsuspected. He was not, however, always so fortunate. Thus, on his arrival at Palencia, he found that the Prior of the convent of that city was a very exact man, who would not be satisfied unless he knew the position and quality of his two guests. Bartholomew found himself greatly embarrassed by the difficulty of satisfying the just demands of the father, and, at the same time, keeping his rank concealed. The

Prior would not be satisfied unless he saw the written permission to travel, of the two fathers, and at length F. Henry de Tavora was obliged to say, "As for me, father, I have no need of a permission; for I have received it from the Archbishop of Braga, who is before you." The Prior was struck dumb with surprise, while Bartholomew's feelings were divided between satisfaction at the exactitude of the Prior and mortification that he should have become known.

On his arrival at the Convent of Burgos his rank passed unnoticed, and as he was pleased with the community, and was besides fatigued with his journey, he resolved to remain there two days to rest. The day after his arrival he sat down in the cloister to spend the after-dinner recreation with the Prior and some of the fathers. At this moment a messenger of the King of Portugal arrived at the convent, loudly inquiring for the Archbishop of Braga. The porter told him that the Archbishop was not there, but only two Portuguese friars who had arrived the day before. The messenger asked no more but hurried into the convent, and at once recognized the Archbishop as he sat amongst the religious. He made him a low reverence, and drew forth the letter he had brought from the king, addressing Bartholomew by his title. The fathers of the convent were, of course, very much surprised, while Bartholomew could hardly help being vexed, as he answered the messenger, "My friend, what made you think of coming to look for the Archbishop of Braga amongst these good fathers?" And then, turning to the Prior, he added, "this man has come here to kill me with his titles! I had begun to enjoy my life, and now he takes it from me!" He had no longer any desire to remain at Burgos, and went away that same day.

He entered Trent on foot, hoping to be quite unnoticed. But his arrival soon became known, and that same evening he was visited by two bishops, both of them Dominicans, who were both equally anxious to receive him into their houses. He became that night the guest of one of these prelates, the Bishop of Modena, who was a man of like spirit to himself, and so given to alms-deeds that he had received the title of "the Father of the Poor."

The work of the great Council of Trent was two-fold. It defined and explained the faith of the Church, more especially on those points which were called in question by the Protestants, and it made many most salutary ordinations relating to the duties and obligations of the clergy. It was in this latter department, that of *discipline*, as it is called, that the influence of Bartholomew was chiefly felt. In the debates on these subjects, the holy fearlessness of his character was especially shown. He was at no time a respecter of persons, and where the interests of God's glory and of the salvation of souls were at stake, nothing could restrain his zeal.

Many examples are related of his uncompromising boldness. Some of the bishops wished to except the Cardinals from the regulations on reform, saying that "the Most Illustrious Cardinals needed no reform." But when it came to Bartholomew's turn to speak, he said, in the most respectful, yet decided manner, "The Most Illustrious Cardinals require a most illustrious reform!" His boldness, however, did not make him enemies. His humility was well known, and it was clearly seen that his plainness of speech proceeded from true apostolic zeal. Thus, the cardinals, who might have taken offence at his plain speaking about them, listened to him without any displeasure, and continued to show him the same marks of confidence and esteem which they had previously.

Throughout the sittings of the Council he continued to speak with a like boldness, and to propose fitting remedies for the evils of the time without respect of persons ; but he always did it with such prudence and sweetness that he gave no offence. Indeed, such was the respect he inspired, that after he had spoken on any subject, many other bishops would rise and say that their opinion was the same as that of the Archbishop of Braga. At length this public expression of confidence in his judgment became so frequent that it distressed his humility ; and when he had expressed his opinion he would at once leave the hall, to avoid such flattering marks of approval.

Most of the measures of reform and discipline that were ordained by the Council were proposed by him, or at least greatly promoted by his energetic support, and especially those relating to the residence of bishops. How momentous were his labors in these respects may be to some extent measured, when we reflect that the Church has now been governed for more than three hundred years by the laws made at this Council, and that for three centuries no other General Council was needed, so amply did it fulfill its purpose. The influence of Bartholomew has, therefore, been felt in the Church for upwards of three hundred years, and continues to live even in our own day.

CHAPTER IV.

BARTHOLOMEW had resolved not to return to Portugal without first visiting Rome. Besides satisfying his devotion, he had other reasons for this, the chief of which was that he wished to resign his see into the hands of the Pope. The burden of his office seemed greater than he could bear; and while others looked on him as the model of pastors, he, in his humility, thought that his unworthiness hindered the reformation of his flock.

A short interruption in the sittings of the General Council gave him the opportunity he sought. He therefore set out for Rome, visiting Bologna on his way, that he might venerate the relics of his spiritual Father, St. Dominic. He prayed to the saint with much fervor and abundance of tears, begging him, amongst other things, that he would obtain for him that he might be delivered from the burden of the episcopate.

On his arrival at Rome, the Portuguese Ambassador, Dom Alvaro de Castro, constrained him, sorely against his will, to stay with him in his palace. Bartholomew himself had wished to be received into the Dominican Convent of the Minerva, among his own religious brethren, but the Ambassador had obtained a command from the Pope that he should either live in the Papal Palace or in that prepared for him. He chose the latter, saying with a graceful courtesy, the effect of a true religious spirit, "I have nothing more to say, my lord, for you have canonized your civility by clothing it with the authority of His Holiness."

Pius the Fourth received him with marked respect, and introduced him to St. Charles Borromeo, saying, "Here is a young man whom I give into your hands; you may begin your church reform upon him." St. Charles no sooner saw Bartholomew than he loved him, and they soon became very close friends. He took an early opportunity of laying open to the Archbishop his whole soul, and consulting him about a very important design which he had for some time had in his mind, namely, that of resigning all his dignities, and leaving the world to retire into some monastery, where, alone with God, he might the more easily save his soul.

Bartholomew could not but admire the generosity of this plan in one so young; moreover, it resembled his own wishes for himself. But he reflected that the possession of honors and dignities had been no temptation to the young cardinal, that they had not weakened his love for God, nor drawn his soul to earthly things, as his present desires plainly showed. Also he thought of the good so ardent a zeal might accomplish for the Church, especially in carrying out the new laws of the General Council. He therefore refused his approval of St. Charles' design, and exhorted him to labor diligently for God's glory in the vast diocese of Milan, of which he had been made Archbishop, and which offered so noble a field for his zeal.

St. Charles submitted to Bartholomew's decision, and thus it may be said that the Church owes to him all that it has gained by the labors and example of the great Archbishop of Milan. On leaving Bartholomew, St. Charles said to him, "You thought that you had come to Rome on your own business, but in truth God sent you to me. By your means He has delivered me from a heavy burden which weighed upon my heart, and has made me see the way in which He wills that I should walk."

And it turned out according as St. Charles had said, for, although Bartholomew implored the Pope to relieve him of the charge of his archbishopric, he did so in vain. When St. Charles heard of it, he rallied him gently on his inconsistency in refusing to him what he desired for himself.

Bartholomew gained at Rome the friendship of another canonized saint. This was the Cardinal of Alessandria, of the Order of St. Dominic, afterwards Pope Pius V.

Our Archbishop met with several occasions, during his short stay at Rome, of showing his boldness of character, and he did not fail to speak his mind, even to the Pope himself. Several instances have been preserved to us; of these we have space for only one; but this one is quite sufficient to show that he spoke and acted quite irrespectively of worldly considerations, when he thought that the honor of God or the good of the Church required him to speak.

One day the Pope took him to see the new buildings he was erecting in the Vatican, in the court of the Belvidere. He then asked him, smiling, for he knew his opinion about such things, why he did not build himself a similar palace at Braga. Bartholomew replied that he had no money to spend in building palaces. "But," said the Pope, "what do you think of these buildings?" "It is for me to admire, Holy Father," said the Archbishop, "and not to judge." "Nay," persisted the Pope, "I wish to have your opinion; and I assure you that I will take in good part whatever you shall say." "Since your Holiness commands me to say what I think," said Bartholomew, "I own that I should find it impossible to build palaces like these, which time will consume, and the Son of God will burn up at the day of judgment. This palace may be well worthy of the architect who has designed it, but it is not worthy of your holiness, whom God has set over His Church to build up living temples for Himself, which will remain when the world shall be destroyed. As for paintings, I own that I only value that which traces on the soul the image of God." The Pope listened with his usual gentleness, and replied, "What can I do? I did not begin these buildings, but I like to finish what have been begun." The Archbishop smiled, and said, "True, Holy Father, good things are still better when they are completed. But the question is, whether God will reckon these buildings among the good works performed by your Holiness." "I see how it is," said the Pope. "You and Charles Borromeo have been together. In you he has found a man according to his own heart. He cares no more for beautiful things than you do; and I will answer for it that the palaces he will build at Milan will be exactly like yours at Braga."

Bartholomew left Rome to return to Trent on October 16th, 1563. The Pope showed him the greatest marks of affection, and presented him, at parting, with a beautiful white mule, which he had hitherto used himself. Poor beast! it led a harder life after entering Bartholomew's service than it had ever done before; for, instead of a splendid stable and little work, it had now to carry its new master first from Rome to Trent, and afterwards from Trent to Braga, where it formed the whole of the Archbishop's stud.

CHAPTER V.

THE Council of Trent concluded its labors' in the year 1563. It had lasted altogether eighteen years, but it had only actually sat five years—two years under Paul III., one year under Julius III., and two years under Pius IV. It was during this last period that Bartholomew had been one of its members, and as soon as the sittings were ended he hastened to return to Portugal, in order that he might resume the care of his flock, from whom he had been separated so long.

On his way home he passed through Avignon. The Vice-Legate of the Pope in that city received him with great honor, and made him acquainted with the following circumstance, which show how beneficial his influence had been during the Council.

Two of the Bishops of that part of France had become infected with some of the heresies prevalent at the time. They had gone to the Council in company, but concealed their errors, on purpose that they might observe the conduct of the prelates of the Church, and oppose them in every possible way. They managed to keep their heresy a complete secret, but they were greatly struck by the conduct of the Bishops who were at the Council. They observed how careful they were to be guided by Holy Scripture and the tradition of the Church, and how far they were from inventing anything of their own, or attempting to introduce anything of human origin into the teaching of the Church. This greatly moved them, and God gave them the grace to renounce the errors they had embraced.

On their return from the Council they made known what had happened to them to the Vice-Legate at Avignon, and to many other persons; and they greatly praised the zeal of many of the Bishops, in the foremost rank of whom they placed the Archbishop of Braga.

Bartholomew arrived in Portugal in February, 1564. The people of Braga were in great joy when they heard of his approaching return, and they prepared a grand public reception for him.

But Bartholomew heard of it in time to avoid it. He entered the city quite privately the night before one of the Sundays in Lent, and astonished his people by appearing in the cathedral pulpit the next day, and making them an exhortation full of zeal and charity.

His first care was to inquire as to what had passed during his absence, how his orders had been observed, and what care had been taken of the poor. Then, before proceeding to any other business, he gave some days to retreat, in order to ask of God the grace to perform all his duties with zeal and prudence.

When this had been done, the first work which he undertook was the foundation of a seminary for the education of the clergy of the diocese, according to the decrees of the General Council at which he had just assisted. For this work he had to make heavy demands upon the incomes of the clergy, and naturally some opposition was made. However, he listened with patience to all the objections and difficulties that were urged, and dealt so gently and prudently with every one that all opposition gave way. As was to be expected, he was himself the largest and most generous contributor.

The work was begun so promptly, and carried on with such vigor, that it was the first seminary opened in Spain or Portugal. Within six months the building was so far completed that there was room for sixty students. The Archbishop soon peopled it with promising subjects, and set over them superiors thoroughly capable of forming them to both learning and piety.

Bartholomew had now to continue the visitation of his vast diocese, which had been interrupted by his journey to Trent. His deep sense of the responsibility of his office, and his inflexibility in accomplishing everything which he believed to be his duty, made this work very difficult, and sometimes very dangerous; for, wherever he detected abuses, whether amongst the clergy or the laity, he was certain to condemn and correct them, and the rank of those who were in fault afforded them no protection whatever from his correction. In this way he made himself many bitter enemies, whom, however, he rarely failed to bring to a better mind by his patience and sweetness. One striking example may be narrated.

There was in the town of Poyarez, which formed part of the diocese of Braga, an important commandery of the Knights of St. John. The Archbishop had heard that the churches which were dependent upon this house were very much neglected, and very ill provided with the necessaries for the worship of God. He therefore determined to make his visitation there, and set in order all that needed reform. That he might have full power to do all that was needful, he obtained special authorization for the purpose from the Pope.

Accordingly he visited these churches, examined diligently into all that they wanted, and took possession of the revenues of the establishment until all that was needful had been supplied.

Now, the Superior, or Commander, as he was called, of this house, was a man of very violent temper, and though now old, was still extremely passionate, and when aroused, his eyes seemed to flame with fire. When he had heard what the

Archbishop had done, his passion was aroused, and he forthwith assembled a band of armed men, and came to the place where the holy prelate was. It was very early in the morning, and Bartholomew was reciting his office when this man abruptly entered the house, and sent word to the Archbishop that he had to speak with him.

Bartholomew replied that he begged him to wait until he had finished his prayers, and meanwhile the Commander paced up and down, his rage increasing with the delay, until at length he sent a second message to the Archbishop, who made him the same answer.

When he had quite finished his office, Bartholomew sent for the Commander and quietly asked him what he wanted with him. The latter, who was boiling with rage, said that he had come to inquire by what authority the Archbishop had acted as he had done on his domain; and then passing to threats, told him that he would teach him to treat a Commander of the Knights of St. John, in a very different manner from the priests and common people of his diocese.

Bartholomew answered him gently, explaining that he had authority for what he had done both from the Council of Trent and from the Pope; and then he pointed out to him that his state of life and his high rank did not exempt him from the law of God and the authority of the Church, but only imposed upon him the duty of greater exactness and fidelity. The Commander was still more enraged at this, and replied with fresh threats of vengeance. The Archbishop made no reply, and did not show by the smallest change of countenance that he felt the outrage which he was suffering. At length he left the room, and went to the church to say mass.

The Commander followed him to the church, still burning with rage and indignation. The Archbishop prayed earnestly for him during the holy sacrifice; and whilst his prayers rose to heaven the grace of God descended upon the unhappy man, gradually enlightening the soul which passion had so blinded. Before the mass was ended the Commander was a changed man, and at its conclusion he went up to the Archbishop, and in the presence of all, confessed his fault and asked pardon.

Bartholomew raised him and embraced him with much tenderness. The Commander promised to provide all his churches with everything that the Archbishop had ordered, and with even greater magnificence, and to perform whatever penance might be imposed upon him. He then went away, full of shame for his faults, giving thanks to God for the mercy that had been shown him. His companions could hardly believe what they saw, and that so great a change could have been accomplished in so short a time. The Commander assured them that it was nothing less than a miracle that had been worked in him by the power of the holy sacrifice and the prayers of the Archbishop. Wherefore ever after he looked on Bartholomew as his father, and never wearied of publishing his virtues and holiness.

This visitation was the means of bringing the grace of God to many other men of rank and position, whom no one with less fortitude than Bartholomew would have dared to reprove for their evil lives.

But still greater good was done to souls by

the Archbishop's visit to the remote mountain districts of his vast diocese, to every nook and corner of which he penetrated. The difficulty of doing so was very great, and not without danger. On one occasion the Archbishop's companions narrowly escaped perishing in a precipice of the mountains of Baroso, and they firmly believed that their preservation was a miracle due to the prayers of the holy prelate.

Churches abounded in these wild mountains, but they were mostly poor and neglected, and very insufficiently provided with sacred vessels. Many of them had chalices only of base metal; all these Bartholomew caused to be destroyed, and he supplied silver chalices in their place at his own expense.

The people were very ignorant, but they were full of faith, and their joy was great at the visit of their Archbishop. They received him with many marks of affection, and he was no less delighted at being with them. When he met parties of them on his way, he would seat himself on a rock and gather them around him, like a father with his children, or a shepherd with his flock; and then he would instruct them with a patience and charity which knew no fatigue. He was extremely anxious to remedy the rudeness and ignorance of these poor people, and he thought that the best means of doing so was to take to Braga a number of the most promising from amongst the children, in order that those amongst them who had the vocation might be trained as priests, aud return to be the pastors of the mountaineers, while the rest might receive a good Christian education, which would make them the means of spreading Christian instruction and manners amongst the rest of the people. This plan was carried out at his expense, with very good results.

CHAPTER VI.

WE have had several occasions to speak of the charity of Bartholomew to the poor. We have now to tell how this virtue displayed itself even to a still greater degree in the extraordinary trials with which his people were afflicted.

In the year 1567, a great famine desolated the kingdom of Portugal. During the preceding years the harvest had been bad, but this year it was much worse. The country people were naturally the first to feel the scarcity, and, finding themselves reduced to great want, they began to flock into the large towns to seek the means of subsistence. Large numbers came to Braga, trusting to find compassion and help from their charitable Archbishop.

Bartholomew was not slow in coming to their assistance. Two noble works were then being carried out by his pious liberality; one was the building of the Jesuit College at Braga, and the other the foundation of a convent of his own order in the busy seaport town of Viana. He at once suspended both these undertakings, in order that he might devote the whole of his means to the relief of the poor, who are the living temples of Jesus Christ. Only a very small part of the revenues of his see had ever been spent on himself or his own household, but he contrived to reduce still more his modest expenditure, for he could not bear that there should be abundance in his house, even of the plainest fare, while there were so many of the poor who lacked the necessaries of life.

The famine was not of short duration. For eight successive years the harvest failed, more especially in those parts of Portugal that lie to the north of the river Douro, where the diocese of Braga is situated. The distress, therefore, was continually increasing. Many died of hunger by the roadside. Bartholomew himself saw a man fall, exhausted by hunger, before his very eyes. Braga was filled with poor, and sometimes as many as three thousand were assembled together at the Archbishop's door, seeking relief.

The holy prelate, who loved discretion in the practice of charitable works, soon saw that, to give effectual help to so vast a number of destitute people, great order would have to be observed. The following system was therefore carried out under his care.

Every day at the Archbishop's dinner hour, towards noon,* a bell was rung, and then all the poor who desired relief entered the palace. A familiar instruction was then given them by some priest, in order to teach them to glorify God in their poverty and trials. They then passed one by one through a door, where stood Father John de Leira, who gave money to each person in proportion to his needs, and according to the number of children in each family, of which he kept careful account. Thence they passed on to a second door, where a priest distributed bread according to the same system, and afterwards to a third, where they received soup and meat.

The Archbishop overlooked the whole pro-

---

* It must be remembered that in southern countries few people take anything to eat until towards the middle of the day.

ceeding from a window, and if it happened that some poor person came late, he would himself call some of his household and have him relieved like the rest, for he could not bear that any one should return sorrowful to his home.

When night was come another class of persons received his aid. These were persons of good station who were suffering from want. They came at night (some of them disguised), that they might not be observed, and Father John de Leira at once gave them privately what was necessary for the support of their family.

This system of relief continued for eight years, until the harvest of 1575, which was very plentiful.

It seems incredible that the revenues of the Archbishop, ample though they were, could have borne such a charge. Nor could they have done so but for his great prudence and careful administration. He foresaw the approaching scarcity, and laid in a very large provision of grain, even borrowing large sums for the purpose.

Moreover, he received much help from rich and charitable people of his diocese, who were roused to zeal both by his example and his words; for the sight of the sufferings of the poor gave great force and energy to his exhortations in the pulpit. He often spoke against the cruelty of those who hoarded up large stores of grain in order to sell it at a high price, thus trafficking in the necessities of the poor, and making them a source of gain. He told the rich that they greatly deceived themselves if they thought that they were in such sort masters of their goods as to be permitted to spend them in useless and foolish expenses; that if God would demand an account of every idle word, much more would he demand an account of wasteful expenditure; and that, after having spent on themselves that which Christian moderation permitted, the rest belonged to the poor. He also told them that if luxury was pernicious and criminal at all times, it was still more so in time of famine; and that a Christian who could see a fellow-Christian weak and dying for want of food without being moved by pity to help him, if he were able to do so, did not deserve to be counted amongst Christians, nor even amongst men.

The miseries of this calamitous time were increased in 1568 by the breaking out of the plague.

It happened that the holy Archbishop was absent from Braga at this time, though he was on his way thither. He received the news that the pestilence had reached Braga with great sorrow, but without surprise or trouble of mind, and at once hastened his return. He was met outside the gates of the city by the magistrates and other chief men, who had come to beg of him not to enter it. They told him that they were most grateful for his charity in coming to them, but that they could suffer no loss so great as to lose him, and that therefore they begged him not to put his life in danger. They said that whilst he lived all those who were devoting themselves to the assistance of the sick would continue their work with courage and confidence, but that if he were to die, they would lose heart, and the whole country would be in desolation.

These were fair reasons, but Bartholomew was not to be persuaded by them. He thanked them for their affection and consideration for him, but he told them that he would rather follow their deeds than their words. They had not thought it enough to give their orders from a distance, but had judged it necessary to remain in the city; how much more, therefore, was not he, their bishop, bound to be in the midst of the sick and dying, since he had the care of their souls and the obligation to encourage the clergy by his example.

The holy Archbishop had no sooner entered the city than with his usual prudence and activity he began to take various measures for the care of the sick and the preservation of the healthy.

His first proceeding was to set in order a large house outside the city walls, and in a very open and healthy spot, to serve as a hospital for the plague-stricken. He sent there a physician and a surgeon, with all the attendants necessary for the service of the sick. He also sent two priests, who were to have the general direction of the hospital and the spiritual charge of the patients, and he ordered them to have a special care of those who were the poorest and most destitute.

He also set apart another house to receive those who were recovering, in order that they might have no communication with the sick.

He then selected a body of men whose duty it was to be to visit the whole of the city in order to find out those who were infected with the plague, and to remove them to the hospital of which we have just spoken, and to bury the dead. It was also their duty to purify the houses where any plague-stricken person had been.

He also took all possible precautions to prevent the pestilence from spreading. He gave directions that the city should be kept in the greatest possible state of cleanliness, and he caused great fires to be kindled in the public squares and streets, as that was thought to be an excellent means for lessening the infection.

Moreover, Bartholomew personally superintended all these matters. Every day he visited both the plague hospital and the house of the convalescents, and himself inquired of the doctors as to the state of their patients, and whether they wanted for anything, and in this way he encouraged every one to zeal and perseverance in the performance of his duties.

The result of Bartholomew's care and watchfulness was most consoling to his charitable heart. Although many of the canons of the cathedral had fled from the city, the parochial clergy remained at their posts without a single exception, and the offices of the church continued to be performed with all the accustomed solemnity, as well as the other extraordinary prayers which the Archbishop had ordered to be said during the time that the pestilence lasted. The poor suffered comparatively little, and, indeed, the city of Braga had much less to endure than other towns of the kingdom. The people were hardly wrong in attributing this mercy to the prayers and labors of their good Archbishop.

CHAPTER VII.

BARTHOLOMEW had never abandoned his ardent desire of resigning his archbishopric and ending his days in the solitude of the cloister, which he had quitted so unwillingly. He had petitioned three successive Popes to grant him this favor, but each, in turn, had refused. When Gregory XIII. became Pope, he resolved to try once more, and this time he was successful.

It may easily be imagined with what sorrow the people of Braga heard that they were to lose their good Archbishop. He had been their pastor for upwards of twenty-three years, during which time he had applied himself without a moment's relaxation to the duties of his office. He had instructed them with marvellous wisdom, and his words had been the light of their souls. He had been the father of the poor, and the consolation of all who were in distress. Large numbers owed their very lives to his charity during the famine and the plague. It is not surprising, therefore, that there should have been universal mourning in Braga when the news of his resignation reached the city.

Meanwhile, Bartholomew lost no time in betaking himself to the Dominican Convent of the Holy Cross at Viana, which he had founded himself, and which was to be the place of his retirement. As soon as he had arrived there, and the religious had come forth to receive him, he cast himself on his knees before the Prior to ask his blessing, and said he had come once more to be received amongst his brethren, with the resolution to regain all that he had lost since he had been absent from conventual life. He then bade farewell to those of his attendants who had come with him, consoling them, and encouraging them to continue to labor faithfully in the service of God.

Bartholomew, finding himself now entirely free from the care of business and from intercourse with the world, gave his whole mind to the work of dying to himself that he might live to God alone. It soon became evident that he had left his archbishopric in order to make himself the least and most abject in the House of the Lord, for he made himself noticeable in the community only by his wonderful humility, modesty, and obedience.

His principal occupations were prayer and the study of the Holy Scriptures; nevertheless, he did not omit to labor for the sanctification of others. As long as his health permitted he went out on foot into the neighboring villages to instruct the simple country people. He continued to do this for three years, and only gave it up when his failing strength made him unequal to the exertion.

The charity towards the poor, for which he had ever been so remarkable, still continued to distinguish him. The Pope, in accepting his resignation of the see of Braga, had obliged him to receive an annual pension out of its revenues. Bartholomew had himself been opposed to this, for he had wished to live in the poverty of a simple religious, but as he was obliged to receive this money, he made use of it to satisfy his charitable desires, and distributed it with great generosity, but at the same time with prudence and discretion, amongst the poor. Some examples have been preserved of his great charity at this period of his life.

As he was returning one Sunday to the convent of Viana, after having preached, according to his custom, in a neighboring village, he was met by a number of poor people. He distributed amongst them all that he had, and then there came up to him a poor woman, already advanced in years, who begged him to give her something. He told her that he was sorry that he could not help her, for he had absolutely nothing left. However, she continued to press him, saying that she had a daughter at home, and that they had not so much as a bed to lie on.

Bartholomew was touched, but he had no money, and did not expect any for some time to come. What could he do? He resolved to give her his own bed, and bethought himself how he could do it without being discovered. He told the mother to come to the convent after dark, and place herself beneath the window of his cell, explaining the exact spot in order that there might be no mistake.

When night came he made up his mattress and bed-clothes into a bundle, and as soon as the woman arrived he thrust it forth to her, and she carried it away rejoicing. Her joy, however, was not so great as that of Bartholomew, who found himself more like our Blessed Lord in not having a bed whereon to rest. It now became his object to hinder its being known in the convent that he was without a bed, for he knew that the want would quickly be supplied if it were discovered. He therefore kept in his cell as much as possible, and if any one came to see him he would not admit him, but went outside to see what was wanted.

The fact at last became known through the woman who had become the recipient of Bartholomew's charity, for she could not help speaking of it to her neighbors, and thus it soon got spread through the town. At length some persons spoke of it to the religious of the convent, thinking that they knew all about it. They were of course very much surprised, and at once understood why Bartholomew had kept his door so carefully closed.

On another occasion a poor countryman applied to him for help; he had lost his yoke of oxen, which formed his only riches. Bartholomew gave him what he had at the moment, which was, however, not enough to repair his loss. A few days after, while he was saying mass, the brother who was serving him noticed that he paused a long time at the memento of the living, and then finished the mass rather quickly. He then left the altar without making his usual long thanksgiving, called his servant, and gave him a considerable sum of money, telling him to go at once to a certain place, where he would meet a poor man carrying a rope, and that he was to give the money to him. The servant did as he was bid; he found the man at the exact place that had been pointed out, and delivered the money to him. It was the very countryman who had lost the yoke of oxen, and who, not having obtained enough money to replace them, had unhappily fallen into despair, and acknowledged that he was then on his way to a retired place in order to commit suicide.

Bartholomew survived eight years after his retirement to the convent of Viana; during the latter half of this period he suffered much from illness. During the summer of the year 1590 his infirmities greatly increased; he concealed them as much as possible, and the religious of the convent remarked only that he rose rather later and retired to rest earlier than was his usual custom, and that he appeared to be extremely weak.

One day at the beginning of July he felt that his illness had greatly increased, and that it would no longer be possible for him to conceal it. However, he made a last effort to say mass, passed a long time in making his thanksgiving and then visited each altar in the church, as if to take a last farewell of the holy place. As he returned to his cell he visited that of F. Andrew of the Cross, who was his especial friend, and said to him, "Father, I am come to let you know my happiness. I think that God has at last granted me that which I have so long asked of

Him. Do not forget to pray for me, for I have great need of it."

He suffered great pain during the last few days of his life, but was so much the master of himself that he allowed no sign of suffering to escape him. His mind remained always fixed on God, and in the midst of his greatest sufferings the only words he uttered were ejaculations of praise and thanksgiving.

It was soon noised abroad that he was dying, and the news reached his successor in the Archbishopric of Braga, Dom Augustin of Jesus, a religious of the order of St. Augustine. This prelate no sooner heard it than he set forth from Braga to visit his dying predecessor, and, traveling all night, he reached Viana the following morning. He remained with Bartholomew until his death, administered to him the sacrament of extreme unction, consoled him with pious thoughts, and rendered him every sort of charitable attention.

Bartholomew received the last anointing with wonderful devotion. He was in perfect possession of his senses, and begged those who were present to help him with their prayers, in order that the sacrament might produce its full effects in his soul. When the penitential psalms were recited, he himself said each alternate verse, and the rest answered. Sometimes it happened that their tears hindered them from saying properly the verse that fell to their turn, and then Bartholomew took it up quite calmly and said it for them.

The Archbishop of Braga recited the recommendation of the departing soul. A few minutes after it was finished Bartholomew raised his hands and his eyes to heaven, aud calmly gave up his soul to God. It was the 16th of July, 1590; he was seventy-six years and two months old.

A controversy soon arose as to the place of his burial. The canons and citizens of Braga demanded that he should be interred in their city, founding their claim upon the fact of his having been their Archbishop. But the inhabitants of Viana strongly protested, alleging that Bartholomew had chosen to end his days and be buried there. The matter was referred to the

Archbishop, who wished to reserve the matter for future discussion, and would have had the convent of Viana receive the sacred remains in deposit, and give them a temporary resting-place. But the Prior of the convent, F. Francis of the Holy Ghost, would by no means agree to receive the body as a deposit only, for the wish of Bartholomew was that he should be buried in that convent, and so the matter was finally decided.

God was pleased to honor his servant by many miracles that were wrought by his intercession. Great numbers of people, therefore, came to visit his tomb, and recommended themselves to his prayers.

About nineteen years after his death his body was removed from its first resting-place to a more sumptuous tomb. The place where it had first been placed was extremely damp; nevertheless, when the grave was opened the body was discovered to be quite entire. Only in one part was the flesh at all decayed; everywhere else it was quite solid and incorrupt, though it had not been embalmed. Moreover, it exhaled a very pleasant odor, which was perceptible to all who were present. This translation took place on May 24th, 1609, on which day is commemorated the translation of St. Dominic, the spiritual father of Bartholomew.

THE VEN. LEWIS OF GRANADA.

THE VEN. LEWIS OF GRANADA.

CHAPTER I.

ALTHOUGH it is chiefly by his learned and pious writings that Father Lewis of Granada is best known, yet the holiness of his life is no less worthy of our admiration than the great knowledge and marvellous talent he shows in his literary works.

This holy religious was born in Granada, a city of Spain, in the year 1505. His father and mother were poor, but descended from a pure Spanish stock, untainted by any Moorish blood. When Lewis was but five years of age his father died, and his pious mother was reduced to the very greatest poverty. She lived near the Dominican Monastery of Holy Cross, and was employed by the Fathers to wash their habits, in order to enable her to eke out her slender living. The good Fathers seeing her merit, took her and her little son under their especial protection, God wishing that Lewis of Granada should be thus bound by ties of gratitude in his youth to that Order which he was destined in after times to enoble by his learning and virtues.

One of his biographers relates that he once had a dispute with some of his play-fellows in the moat of the town citadel. Blows followed words, and a fight took place under the eyes of the governor, the Count of Mondejar, who was walking on the ramparts at the time. He sent some soldiers to separate the youthful combatants. Lewis, who had not begun the fight, begged them to take him before the Count, to whom he explained the whole matter, and justified himself with such spirit and grace of manner, that the Count took a liking for him, and after making inquiries about his family, made him the companion and fellow-student of his own sons, sending him to college with them, and taking upon himself the whole charge of his education.

Lewis at once showed himself worthy of the Count's generosity. His masters saw his wonderful natural gifts, and his studious habits. His memory was extraordinary. During Lent, having, in company with his benefactor's family, attended a course of sermons preached by one of the Dominican Fathers, on his return to the Count's house each evening, he repeated the whole sermon without forgetting a single passage, and imitating the action and gestures of the preacher so perfectly as to exactly reproduce him.

His piety and natural abilities were so well known in Granada that when he offered himself to the Dominican Fathers as a novice he was at once accepted, and was clothed with the Dominican habit on June 15th, 1524. During his noviciate he showed himself humble, modest, exact in all his duties, and above all, very docile to the instructions of his novice master. He never failed in his duties, observed the least points of the rule with perfect fidelity; and all his biographers say that for the whole sixty-eight years of his religious life he never lost his first fervor, and ever preserved the same love for the monastic rule which he had showed in his noviciate.

At the end of the year the fathers gladly allowed him to make his profession and take the religious vows; for he had given so many and solid proofs of true virtue, and had shown signs of such great powers of mind, that there could be no doubt as to his vocation. He performed this great act of his life with such joy and enthusiasm that all present were much edified.

After a course of philosophy, in which he did not disappoint the expectations formed of him, he was sent to the convent of Valladolid to study theology. This was a sad blow for him: he feared for his mother, with whom, since his entrance into the Order, by permission of his superiors, he had always shared his dinner, dividing his portion in the refectory into two, the larger of which he sent to her; and he was now afraid that poverty would severely pinch her in his absence. But just as he was setting off on his journey, he learned that the Count of Mondejar, his kind benefactor, had taken her under his charge, and would not let her want for anything.

His love for his mother was one of the most beautiful traits in his character; he was never ashamed of her on account of her poverty, and often visited her in her humble home. He once gave a very striking proof of it which we cannot omit here, although it took place years later. One day as he was preaching to a large audience of rich people, he saw that his mother, being a poor woman, had been forced to remain near the church doors, where he knew she would scarcely be able to hear his sermon. He paused, and pointing her out, said, "I pray you let that poor woman pass, she is my mother." At once all made way for her, and ladies of the highest rank offered to give up their places to the humble widow.

At Valladolid, Lewis continued the same wise union of study with prayer, dividing his time between these two duties with rare fervor. He dived deep into the most abstruse questions of theology, showing great penetration and sagacity. No subtlety seemed an obstacle to him; he seized at once what his professors taught him, and quickly made it his own. He early formed a strong preference for mystical theology, God not only giving him a great liking for it, but also clear light which enabled him to search into its most secret and profound mysteries. It was about this time that he first conceived the plan of several of his works, and began to make extracts from all the books he read, arranging them in order under different headings. It is to this that we must attribute the richness and variety of the quotations which distinguish his writings.

He did not omit to mortify his body by severe penances and disciplines. He chose a cell at the end of the dormitory, in order to be able to practice his bodily mortifications unseen and unheard. There he gave himself the discipline for whole hours, making a bloody sacrifice of his body to make himself more like to Jesus crucified. But he was found out in a way that would never have been expected. Two young gentlemen of the town were going in the silence of the night to a bad house, in order to gratify their sinful desires. It was eleven o'clock, the street was deserted and silent, but passing under the convent windows, they heard the rapid and measured sound of the scourge descending upon the back of Brother Lewis, and heard his sighs and groans. They drew near the window and listened for some time. Divine grace softened their hearts; they could not help contrasting the heroism of this man living in holiness, and yet so severe to himself, with their own sensual and sinful life, and were seized with a profound horror for the sin they were about to commit. The next morning, as Brother Lewis was studying in his cell, the two young gentlemen entered, fell at his feet, told him what had happened, and with tears in their eyes besought him to pray that God would pardon them their sinful deeds. Thus God shows us how he uses the penances and mortifications of His saints for the conversion of sinners. Those who lead a life of self-indulgence often ask to what purpose are all the fasts, midnight watches, and painful disciplines of contemplative religious. This beautiful incident answers them. Again and again we read in the lives of the saints how sinners have been turned from their evil ways by the austerities of some holy man. Yet the instances that are thus recorded must be, of course, few compared with the great number which have occurred, and are known to God alone. Surely the world in general has every reason to desire that they who have embraced a life of penance may continue with courage their course, and thus expiate the sins of the self-indulgent, and earn for them the grace to repent, before it is too late.

CHAPTER II.

AFTER several years of theological studies' at Valladolid, Lewis returned in 1534 to the Convent of the Holy Cross at Granada, where he was ordained priest, and said his first Mass. His superiors wished him to teach philosophy and theology, but he felt strongly drawn to preaching, and asked to be allowed to devote himself exclusively to the salvation of souls.

It was in the church of his Convent at Granada that he began his course as a preacher, which he continued as long as he lived. At once he drew all the city to hear him; but he was not merely a popular preacher whom all went to hear from custom or fashion, but a converter of souls. His words were so forcible and true, and his life was so exactly conformable to what he preached, that innumerable conversions followed his sermons. All looked upon him as an apostle sent from God, and regarded him as a saint, who showed in his own holy life a beautiful example of the innocence and love of God which he preached to others. Writers of his life liken him to a silkworm, for, they quaintly observe, as the silkworm, after having fed upon juicy leaves, becomes filled with nourishment and draws from its own substance the silk which it provides for the good of men; so Father Lewis, after having stored his mind and strengthened his own soul by reading the Holy Scriptures, poured forth for the salvation of souls rich treasures of knowledge and wisdom, scattering them abroad in the hearts of men. He had all the external qualities required for a good preacher—a clear and ringing voice, clear enunciation, and commanding presence; and the graces God gave to his soul were no less favorable to success. He had a precious unction, great powers of persuasion, and, above all, the gift of placing himself, at once, and as if by instinct, on a level with his audience. For forty years he filled the churches of Spain with his Christ-like eloquence, preaching in the humblest country churches as well as in the most splendid cathedrals, only leaving the pulpit to enter the confessional, there to complete the conversion of those sinners whom he had touched by his words, and to give back to God souls freed from sin by his priestly absolution.

When he was forty years of age, after several years of apostolic labors, his superiors, thinking that he needed rest, sent him to restore the Convent of Scala Cœli, at Cordova. It had been founded in the preceding century by Blessed Alvarez, of the Order of Friar Preachers. For a long time it was the home of saints, and a model of strict religious observance; but owing to poverty, and, as some writers say, to the unhealthy situation, the fervor of its inmates had sadly fallen off, and it stood in great need of reform. The buildings also, which had fallen into a state of dilapidation, owing to want of means, required many repairs. The decline of this once fervent community is an illustration of St. Teresa's maxim, that too great poverty is a worse evil for a religious house than too great riches. Father Lewis at once set about his difficult task, and soon effected the desired reform. He established strict observance of the rule, and begged from the people of Cordova sufficient to repair the cells and cloisters, thus completely satisfying the wishes of his superiors, by the spiritual and material reparation of the convent.

The Convent of Scala Cœli was built upon a hill, at some distance from the city, but this did not hinder the people from going to hear his sermons. Nearly every week he preached in the convent church, and often in the city, with the same wonderful effect as at Granada, and many were those he led back to God.

One Good Friday, he took a missal with him into the pulpit, and opening it, read out these words, "The Passion of our Lord Jesus Christ." Then closing the book, he began his sermon in this wise: "Can there be one among you who has not the passion of Jesus Christ deeply graven upon his heart? Of what use, then, can this book be to you? seeing that each of you can reproduce the passion of our Lord from his own soul. Listen then, oh my brothers, and let us together bewail the infamy of man's sins, which nailed the Saviour of the world upon the cross.'

Then he set himself to paraphrase the whole of the Passion, from the Garden of Olives to Calvary, with such force and fervor, that sobs, tears, and agonizing cries burst forth from all parts of the church. It was impossible to finish the sermon, and he was obliged to leave the pulpit, himself bathed in tears, and thanking God for having given such power to his words.

It was at Cordova that Father Lewis wrote his first book. The quiet and solitude of the convent enabled him to devote more time to writing than he would have been able to do had he continued his apostolic journeys among the towns and villages of Spain. His first work was the celebrated "Treatise on Prayer and Meditation." Nicolas Antoine, a learned author, says of this work that of "all books of its kind, in any tongue or of any time, it deserves the first place." It soon became famous, and was even read by the Mahometan inhabitants of Spain, deadly enemies to Christianity as they were. In his preface to "The Introduction to the Creed," a later work, he himself tells how it worked the conversion of one of those infidels, a Moorish slave, called Hamelsi, who, touched by grace, after reading the "Treatise on Prayer," asked for baptism, and became a pious Christian.

During his sojourn at Cordova he was called to assist at the Provincial Chapter, which was held in the domains of the Duke of Medina-Sidonia. While there he was asked to preach in the presence of the Duke, who was so pleased with his sermon that he not only requested that the manuscript be given him, but also that Father Lewis might remain in his dukedom, and thus be able to live near him. The Provincial acceded to his wishes; but, after he had preached several sermons there, and acquired a very high reputation, he was sent to Badajoz, where the Provincial wished him to found a new monastery of his Order. The moral state of Badajoz was very bad when he arrived there; most of its inhabitants were neglectful of their religious duties, and it was the few who had preserved their fervor who had invited the Dominican Fathers to come to aid in the sanctification of the town.

Father Lewis arrived there in the year 1554, and at once commenced preaching the great truths of the Christian faith. The church was almost empty at his first sermon, but the people soon came in crowds to hear him, and the seed of the Holy Word, thrown into soil long untilled, yet still fertile, fructified, and produced a full harvest of consoling conversions. While at Badajoz he wrote his precious book called "The Guide," or rather, as it should be translated, "The Bridle of Sinners." This energetic and striking book has been the means of touching the hearts of thousands of evil livers, who have been led back to the feet of God by reading it It has been translated into Latin, Greek, Italian, French, German, English, Polish, Persian and Chinese.

The fame of Father Lewis of Granada had by this time spread from one end of Spain to the other, and had even reached the neighboring kingdom of Portugal. Everywhere the holy preacher was in demand: all wished to hear him, and he was forced to give way to the powerful influence of the Cardinal Don Henry, son of King Emmanuel of Portugal, and brother to King John III., who wished him to go and live at Evora, of which place he was Archbishop. This royal Cardinal, who afterwards ascended the Portuguese throne, had chosen the ecclesiastical state in his youth. He lived in his see, and gave an example to all around him of the highest virtue. He said Mass every day, and with his own hand distributed the Bread of Life to his flock. He heard the confessions of all who wished to come to him, baptized children, visited the sick, carried the Holy Viaticum to them himself, gave large alms to the poor, and in no way claimed a dispensation from his duties as a priest and Archbishop on account of his rank.

As soon as he heard of the arrival of Father Lewis at the Dominican Convent at Evora, he went to him, and, entering his cell, knelt down and asked him to hear his confession; but Father Lewis answered, "Will your royal highness be pleased to excuse me, for, as I am a stranger to the diocese, I should ill justify the confidence placed in me if I were to undertake the direction of your conscience before I knew if there were any crimes or public scandals which it is your duty to remove."

The Cardinal admired the wisdom of his answer, and, instead of taking offence, put himself entirely under his guidance, gave him every facility for knowing the state of his diocese, and followed his advice in all things. He determined not to lose the treasure he had found in Father Lewis, and wished him to be affiliated to the convent of Evora. This was much opposed by the Fathers of the Spanish province, as they did not wish to give him up. However, the Portuguese Dominican Fathers elected him their Provincial, two years later—that is to say, in the year 1557.

He fulfilled his new duties with wonderful prudence, mixed with kindness and consideration for those over whom he was placed. Above all, he astonished them by the way in which he contrived to find time for study and prayer, without in the least neglecting his duties as Provincial; and it is told of him that, when he went from one monastery to another to make his visitation, he contrived a little desk, which he fixed upon the saddle of the mule on which he rode, so that he could read or write with ease, and not be forced to lose so many golden hours in mere traveling. It was during these apostolic journeys that he translated the "Spiritual Ladder of St. John Climacus" from Latin into Spanish.

CHAPTER III.

THE kingdom of Portugal was ruled at that time by Catharine, Queen Regent, widow of John III., brother of Cardinal Henry. This royal lady, who was even more remarkable for her true and solid piety than for her exalted rank, formed a high esteem for Father Lewis, and not content with making him her confessor, always consulted him upon state affairs of importance. Thinking that a man of such holiness and merit deserved the rank and position of a ruler of the Church, for which he showed very marked qualifications, she offered him the bishopric of Viseu, and not discouraged by his refusal to accept that dignity, again attempted to raise him to the episcopal dignity, when the Archbishopric of Braga became vacant by the death of Dom Balthazar Limpo in 1558; and this time would not readily accept his refusal.

"Father Lewis," she said in a sharp and commanding tone, "I charge you with the Archbishopric of Braga. You must either accept it yourself, or find a man truly fit for the office. For my part, my conscience is free from this burden, and I put upon your shoulders the obligation of providing a worthy bishop for this see. In three days you must give me your final answer." She then dismissed him with a dryness and severity not usual to her, in which all the courtiers thought they saw a firm determination to make him accede to her design.

The holy friar spent the three days in prayer, hardly eating or sleeping, and asking God to show him upon whom His choice fell. At the end of the time he went to the Queen, who said: "I hope, Father, that your reflections are made, and that you accept." "Madam," answered Father Lewis, "allow me to say once more that I feel myself unworthy of so high a post. I have recommended this affair to God, who has secretly inspired me to say that if the choice fell upon Father Bartholomew of the Martyrs, your conscience, as well as my own, would be free from regret upon this point." "Alas, Father Lewis," answered the Queen, "I see you make too low an estimation of your virtue; you truly grieve me; but the sorrow you cause me as Regent, redoubles the admiration and respect I have for you as a Christian. Go and make known to Father Bartholomew that he is now Archbishop of Braga."

This choice was, as he nimself said, an inspiration from on high, for the name of the Venerable Bartholomew of the Martyrs is that of a perfect model of a true and indefatigable bishop. Father Lewis had some difficulty in persuading him to take upon himself the burden, but at last succeeded. He always proved a faithful adviser to the Archbishop, and two years later paid him a visit at Braga, accompanied by Father Bernard of the Cross, another Dominican Bishop, who had resigned the see of Saint Thomè, to return to the cloister. Nor can we be sorry that Father Lewis did not illustrate the episcopate by his virtues, for by remaining a simple religious he was able to write those excellent books which have proved of such use to all who walk in the paths of holiness.

Soon after this he consented to found a convent of the Dominican Order at Viana, eighteen miles from Braga, which the Archbishop proposed to him. This town was celebrated for its flourishing trade and wealth, but also for the careless and irreligious lives of its people. It was a seaport, and had all a seaport's vices. Men of all nations were to be found in it, who had brought thither the evil habits of all countries. By founding a convent of his brethren in religion, the holy Archbishop hoped by their good example and the force of their preaching to infuse a new spirit into this town. Father Lewis readily entered into his views, and himself went to establish it. It was dedicated to the Holy Cross, and fully answered the expectations with which the Venerable Archbishop had founded it. In later years it had the privilege of receiving the holy prelate, when he retired from his see, for it was there he passed the last years of his life, and was buried.

By this time the fame of Father Lewis had spread throughout Europe, and he was admired and consulted by men of the highest rank, both in Church and State. The King of Spain and many cardinals and bishops honored him with marks of great esteem. St. Charles Borromeo, Cardinal-Archbishop of Milan, although he had never seen him, wrote to him, and used his books as a storehouse of matter for preaching. Another eminent cardinal, Michael Bonelli, nephew of Pope Pius V., who was Papal Legate in Portugal, was so much impressed by his virtues and by his works, that he several times sent him money to be given away in alms among the poor. Pope Gregory XIII. addressed a brief to him, dated July 21st, 1582; it was written at the suggestion of St. Charles Borromeo, and praises in high terms the works of the holy religious and his apostolic labors among the people, and adds that his sermons, like his writings, merit him a precious crown in heaven, because having labored with such striking success to draw sinners from their disorders and from the darkness of ignorance, he was not less favored by God than if he had had the power to give sight to the blind and life to the dead.

A few years later Pope Sixtus V. wished to raise him to the rank of cardinal, but Father

Lewis hastened to tell His Holiness that he was eighty years of age, and so infirm that he could not leave his cell, and therefore unfit for the duties of so high a position.

All these honors and marks of esteem did not cause any pride in his heart; he had long ago trodden under foot all earthly desires, when he put on the lowly habit of the sons of St. Dominic, and had never lost his first love for holy poverty and humility. Pressed one day by another religious to wear a habit less worn and patched than that which he commonly used, he said: "Oh, my dear brother, I am clothed better than I desire. When I was a boy I had nothing but rags, and ran about the town barefooted, following my poor mother. We often went to the convent at Granada to beg an alms. I carried a little pot in my hands, into which the brothers put a little soup and some scraps, and we were happy to receive so much." And this was a man consulted by crowned heads, whom kings and cardinals felt proud to call their friend, and to whom the Vicars of Christ offered the purple!

CHAPTER IV.

BUT we must take up our narrative again at the time when Father Lewis refused the see of Braga. In 1561, having finished his provincialate, he was sent to Lisbon at the wish of Queen Catharine, where he spent his time in preaching and writing several works, which he published there. But neither his many occupations nor his age hindered him from keeping the monastic rule. He sang the praises of God in the choir with the other religious, although his age and literary labors entitled him to many dispensations.

His daily life was as follows:—He rose at four o'clock. From that hour until six he was occupied in prayer and meditation. At six he said Mass, at seven he either read himself or listened to some one who read to him. From eight till ten he dictated to a secretary, then wrote with his own hand until eleven, when he dined in the refectory with the community.

When dinner was over he either visited the sick or joined in the common recreation; after which he took a short rest, according to the custom of most hot countries. At two he again set to work, and dictated until complin, which was either at seven or eight, according to the season. After this he meditated and prayed for a couple of hours, and then read a spiritual book for an hour. At eleven he cooked two eggs over his lamp, in order not to give any trouble to the lay brothers; and, after he had eaten them, went to bed. He thus spent almost the whole day and night in prayer, meditation, and study. He looked upon solitude and silence as the best safeguard for innocence of body and soul; yet he did not complain when his superiors sent him out of the convent to hear confessions, visit the sick, or preach. He went willingly, gave just time enough to finish the work for which he was sent, and then hastened back to his beloved convent home.

His cell was of the poorest, furnished with two chairs, a plain wooden table, aad a poor bedstead, covered with the cast-off habits of the other religious. A rude crucifix, and some common paper pictures of our Blessed Lady and his own patron saints, hung upon the wall. Once, when he was ill in his convent, Cardinal Albert, hearing that he was destitute of all comforts, sent him a present of a mattress, thick warm bed clothes, and half-a-dozen holland shirts; but it was useless: he was so firmly wedded to bodily mortification that he no sooner saw them than he sent them to the convent infirmary.

His spirit of prayer was very remarkable. He spent three or four hours every day in sweet converse with God, now kneeling, now prostrate upon the ground, now with his arms spread out in the form of a cross; and when he had satisfied his soul with prayer, he failed not to imitate Saint Dominic, by giving himself long and severe disciplines. He could not understand how anyone could say the divine office with coldness or indifference. One night he saw a friar asleep during the Psalms of Matins. "Brother," he said sweetly, "he who prays to God should be watchful and attentive."

He said Mass daily, unless prevented by illness. He appeared as if in ecstacy all the time, especially at the Canon and Consecration; and his devotion was so great that a large crowd always assisted at it in order to have a share in the spiritual blessing which God then poured out upon his soul. "To say Mass well, to-day," he once said, "is the best preparation for tomorrow's Mass." After Mass, he always liked to be left alone, to make his thanksgiving, face to face with that God who was then dwelling in his heart.

Father Lewis was always ready to help and counsel those who were striving to lead a holy life. He watched them carefully, took note of all their attempts to put down evil inclinations, and to cherish and improve what was noble and good in their natural character. He wrote out all he saw of good among those who lived with him, and made use of what he thus acquired to write a book called "Lives of Illustrious and Holy Men of our Own Age." One of those whose virtues he thus narrated was the Venerable Bartholomew of the Martyrs. But if he studied the acts, the wisdom, and the courageous and persevering struggles and progress of the truly pious and good, so that he might be edified by them, he also had occasion to tremble when he saw how, in many cases, the wiles of the devil led souls astray. One wretched slave of Satan put himself under the direction of Father Lewis on purpose to deceive him. He showed outward signs of sorrow for his sins, and loudly professed his wish to advance in the spiritual life; but his real intentions were full of iniquity. At first Father Lewis was deceived, but soon detected the fraud. He shed floods of tears over this man's hypocrisy, and undertook unheard of penances to expiate his sins.

It is thought that it was this sad incident which led him to publish a sermon on the text of St. Paul, "Who is weak, and I am not weak? Who is scandalized, and I burn not?" His idea in publishing it was to encourage souls in the practice of solid virtue, and to teach them not to be cast down when they see the evil examples of those who chose a life of earthly pleasure, neglecting the life of the soul. He took great pains with this sermon, and spent the whole Advent of the year 1588, the last of his life, in revising it.

He had suffered much from a painful illness for more than two years, and, towards the close of 1588, all saw that he had not long to live. Yet he did not wish to diminish any of his fasts or penances, and it was a grief to him to think that he could not keep the rule like the other religious. One day, the Father who had charge of him in his illness, thinking of the loss his Order and the Church would suffer by his death, which he knew could not be far distant, broke into tears near the bed where the holy man lay. "Come, my brother," said Father Lewis to him, "do not grieve; you see that I do not weep. Rejoice that I am leaving this sad world, this place of pilgrimage and woe, to go to my heavenly home, to our Blessed Lady, the angels and saints, and to see the face of God. Dry your tears then, my good Father, because I am happy, being sure that God will receive me into paradise, where I will not fail to pray for you.' He bore his sufferings with great patience, and underwent the most severe attacks with all the calm of a martyr, continually raising his eyes to heaven, and breathing forth ardent aspirations to be freed from the ties which yet bound him to earth. Two days before his death, the proof sheets of the sermon of which we spoke above were brought him, and the last act of his life was to revise them.

On New Year's Eve the doctors warned him that he had but a few hours to live. It was truly joyful news to him; and joining together his hands, he cried out in a voice which his delight made strong and clear, like that of a young and healthy man, "At last I am going into the house of the Lord. Blessed and happy for ever and ever are they who go there."

He for the last time received the body and blood of his Lord with such reverence, humility, and radiant joy, that for a time those who stood by forgot the grief of parting in admiration of his holiness. Kneeling near the bed were all his brethren; one of them, the master of novices, arose, and drawing near, asked him, "Have you strength enough, Father, to say a few words to our young brothers, the novices, to inspire them in aiming at becoming one day what you yourself have been, worthy sons of St. Dominic?" Father Lewis answered, "If I have not the strength of myself, God will give it to me." The novices drew near, and stood around the bed; then, all on fire with divine love, he spoke to them, exhorting them to keep great purity of conscience, to be active and fervent in the service of God, and to labor with courage and perseverance for the glory of the Order which they had entered. He spoke easily, without showing signs of fatigue, and ended with these words: "Be attentive to your duties, and faithful to the rule, my dear children; fulfill exactly the obligation of your vows. Above all, never lose sight of the crown in heaven, which will more than repay you for your efforts and perseverance. Think how short life is, in comparison with a happy eternity, where God will give you the grace, as I firmly hope, to rejoin me there." Then, taking a last farewell of all present, he asked to be left alone, and for forty minutes remained plunged in silent ecstacy, calling forth all the powers of his soul to unite him to his Saviour, who was speedily coming to receive him.

He received the sacrament of Extreme Unction at four o'clock in the afternoon, after which he asked that the Passion of our Lord, according to St. John, might be read to him. He listened to every word attentively, holding a lighted candle in his hand, already chilled by death, saying that the light was an image of the faith which he had always been so happy as to possess from his birth, and which he still preserved at the hour of his release from this world. Towards nine in the evening his agony began; and as the Fathers chanted the prayers for the dying, he gave up his soul to God. It was December 31st, 1588. He was then eighty-four years old.

The next day his body was carried into the church, and a great crowd of people came to see him for the last time, to kiss his feet, or to obtain some grace by his merits before God. The following day all the town reassembled to assist at the funeral service, and to hear the panegyric which was preached by a famous preacher of the Dominican Order, Father Anthony de Soza, who afterwards became Bishop of Viseu.

The life of Father Lewis of Granada was written shortly after his death by Father Francis Diego, who says that he had heard all he wrote of him from Father Francis Oliveyra, who had lived many years in the same convent with Father Lewis, reading to him, and writing what he dictated; assisted him in his old age and last illness. Many other lives of him have been written in several European languages and in Latin. Father Seraphin Razzi, who wrote his life in Italian, thus concludes his work: "If anyone ask me if Father Lewis of Granada ever worked any miracles, I answer him what Pope John XXII. answered the Consistory of Cardinals when they asked if St. Thomas Aquinas had worked a miracle, that every article he wrote, and he wrote 1554, in his opinion was a miracle.* I also say that

---

* NOTE.—It must not from this be inferred that St. Thomas did not work any miracles; on the contrary, he worked many, both during life and after death.

which a great preacher of our Order, Father Michael de Rozel, was accustomed to say, 'that as St. Thomas came into the world to enlighten our understanding, so Father Lewis of Granada came into the world to set our wills on fire.' It may be said truthfully that each chapter of his works is a miracle."

It now only remains to give a short account of what he wrote, for it is as a writer that he is chiefly known. In addition to the "Treatise on Prayer and Meditation." his first work, "The Introduction to the Creed," and "The Guide for Sinners," which we have already mentioned, he wrote "The Memorial of a Christian Life," a work on "Christian Doctrine," a learned and very useful book called "The Christian Orator," which he supplemented by a collection of matter for preachers, called "Sylva Locorum Communium," a golden little work on "The Office and Duties of Bishops," "A Dialogue on the Incarnation," "The Catechism Abridged," the collection of lives to which we have alluded in the course of this life, "A Moral Philosophy," and some other small treasures. His sermons fill several volumes, and he translated various works from the Latin, such as part of the "Imitation of Christ," which he called "The Contempt of the World," and "The Spiritual Ladder of St. John Climacus."

We cannot do better than conclude this sketch of his life in the words of St. Francis of Sales, who, writing to a Bishop, one of his friends, says: "Have by you Lewis of Granada entire. Let him be your second breviary. St. Charles Borromeo had no other theology to preach but Lewis of Granada, yet he preached very well; but this is not his principal use; it is that he will form your mind to the love of true devotion and all spiritual exercises necessary for you. My wish is that you begin to read him with the great 'Guide for Sinners,' that you then pass on to the 'Memorial,' and, in fine, that you read all he wrote. But to read him with fruit you must not run through him hastily; he must be pondered, and have his full weight, and chapter after chapter must be mused upon and applied to the soul with much thought and prayer to God. You must read him with reverence and devotion, like a book containing the most useful inspirations man can receive from on high, and thereby reform all the powers of the soul." (Letter of 3d of June, 1603.)

A complete translation of all his works into French, in twenty-two volumes, was published in Paris in the year 1866. It is to be hoped that ere long some one will give us a similar work in English, for the translations of the "Sinner's Guide" and the "Memorial" which we have, do not worthily represent the originals.

BY THE SAME AUTHOR:

The Life of the Angelic Doctor, St. Thomas Aquinas. Small octavo, $1.00. A large reduction made in price to those who take a quantity.

Manual of the Confraternity of the Girdle of St. Thomas Aquinas, for the preservation of Chastity. 15 cents.

Copies of these works sent free by mail on receipt of price.

Address Rev. FATHER J. A. DYSON, O. P., St. Dominic's Monastery, Benecia, Solano Co., Cal., from whom also Girdles of St. Thomas may be obtained. Price 10 cents.